Conversations with the Old Testament

LEARNING CHURCH

Conversations with the Old Testament

John Holdsworth

scm press

© John Holdsworth 2016

Published in 2016 by SCM Press

Editorial office
3rd Floor, Invicta House,
108–114 Golden Lane,
London EC1Y 0TG, UK

SCM Press is an imprint of Hymns Ancient & Modern Ltd
(a registered charity)
13A Hellesdon Park Road, Norwich,
Norfolk NR6 5DR, UK

www.scmpress.co.uk

British Library Cataloguing in Publication data

A catalogue record for this book is available
from the British Library

978 0 334 05401 6

Typeset by Regent Typesetting
Printed and bound by
CPI Group (UK) Ltd, Croydon

Contents

To Lewys John Holdsworth *gyda chariad*

Introduction:
Apologetic, not Apology

The term 'apologetic' is strangely out of vogue. In my view that is a shame because I believe it is an essential skill for anyone concerned with any kind of Christian ministry, and a definite responsibility for anyone writing a book about the Old Testament. By apologetic I mean the art of describing something in a persuasive way, and quite subjectively, from conviction that it matters. What the writer of an Old Testament introduction has to do is not necessarily persuade people to accept the faith claims of the Old Testament, but persuade them that this is a volume worth taking notice of: something that has a contribution to make to a number of current social, political, ethical and pastoral issues. Discussion of the Old Testament needs to be in the public arena. And so I title the book *Conversations with the Old Testament*.

Most books about the Old Testament are not conversations, or at least if they are, they are pretty one-sided. Writers write as if they have an avid audience, wanting above anything to find out more about the structure, history and message of the Old Testament, when the reality is that most people, even in faith communities, will have to be persuaded to open such a book in the first place. And so only those who must study the Old Testament as part of a course are likely naturally to seek out books of introduction to these texts. What as much as anything attracts me to write for the Learning Church series is a sense that the teaching and learning methods it embraces acknowledge the same frustrations about the narrowness of conventional teaching as I feel. I want people to be able to read these texts not just to pass an exam, not just to learn more about ancient cultures, not because they are religious geeks but because they want to see how pastorally, socially and politically useful these texts can be and how they can aid what might loosely be called 'discipleship'.

The understanding behind this book is that the conversation begins in the real world of the present and consists of a mild interrogation of the texts to see what light they throw on a series of contemporary issues. These vary from the real concerns aroused by the debate around creationism and the roots of conflict in the Middle East crisis, to more personal but pressing questions in our denial-based society about the reality of suffering and pain. Each chapter identifies a credible questioner with a credible question. It is my hope that in the process of giving a response, the most important critical issues of Old Testament study will nonetheless be covered, and that at the end of the process the reader will not only know more about the Old Testament and the history of its critical scholarship but will also have a chance to reflect on the question, in each case, and the response to it.

There are some basic facts that have to be set out in any introduction and I want to get those out of the way, so here goes.

The 39 books of what Christians call the Old Testament were and are known to Jews as a collection in three parts: Law, Prophets and Writings. Those descriptions will mean nothing much to us in terms of content: the Prophets section does not only include what we might recognize as prophecy; and to describe a section as Writings is to state the obvious – but that division does tell us something about the way the collection came together. The first section, the Law, comprising the first five books of the Old Testament, was the first to be published, shortly after the Exile, probably in the fifth century BC. (The Exile was the great disaster that befell the people of Judah when their country was conquered by the Babylonians and then, in two waves, most of the inhabitants were taken as slaves to Babylon. This happened in 597 and 587 BC. After Babylon was conquered, in turn, by the Persians, people could return to Jerusalem, and some did from 539 BC onwards.) The second section, the Prophets, had been published by 180 BC – we know that because of a reference in a book of that date. So by the time of Jesus, people could refer to their holy writings as the Law and the Prophets. The third section, the Writings, were added towards the end of the first century AD. (Yes, that does mean that the Old Testament did not reach its final form until after most of the New Testament had been written.)

To give publication dates is not to describe the date of the material contained in the books. For the most part the different sections contain books from different eras and, even within those books, material from different eras, some of it very ancient. Among the genres of writing we find quite a lot of *narrative*; that is, storytelling. There are many *prophetic oracles*; that is, the declarations made by people – usually men – publicly, claiming them to be the immediate word of God. There is a whole section of Psalms; that is, *liturgical materials* used in worship, together with other liturgical material and instructions about how to conduct liturgy. There is a deal of reflective material, sometimes called *Wisdom literature*, dealing with diverse subjects, based on observation of the human condition. In addition there are sections that are almost impossible to read, consisting of *long lists* of genealogies, temple furnishings or other apparently uninteresting things.

The story the Old Testament wants us to read has as its backbone a story about a particular people in society, a nation, with whom God had a special relationship with an agreement that had responsibilities on both sides, called the Covenant. We read about the antecedents of this society and how it eventually came to be formed in its own land following the liberation of slaves from Egypt, who made a long journey (Exodus) across the desert to reach it, enter it and settle it. We read about the vicissitudes of the society in good times and bad, until the fateful exile. Briefly, we read about the task of those who returned from exile, but the society they manage is a pale reflection of the land in its heyday, and the people are left wanting more.

I say 'the story the Old Testament wants us to read' advisedly, since some modern scholarship believes we should question that and try to get behind it, asking why it is presented in the way it is.

But this collection of writings does not have one party line. In some places there is repetition, with different approaches to the same material. This is most noticeable in two distinct tellings of the history of Israel: one that extends from Joshua to 2 Kings, and the other that is told in 1 and 2 Chronicles, Ezra and Nehemiah. We shall see the significance of this in due course.

It is probably true to say that no branch of theological studies has seen such development and interest over the past 30 years as Old Testament study. To enter the field now is to be part of an adventure as well as a conversation. May it be so for you.

1

What does the Bible mean when it says that God created the world?

Meet Richard. He is a young teacher with a Physics degree. He is also a regular attender at his local church. When this latter fact became known to his head teacher, he was encouraged to augment his science teaching with a couple of lessons of religious education because the school was short of dedicated RE teachers. Richard agreed. He now finds himself in a quandary, having to face questions he has up to now been able to ignore.

Until now Richard has been able to regard his churchgoing as a natural extension to his personality without having to examine too deeply the doctrinal basis of faith claims. But as a teacher, and especially as a science teacher, he is beginning to wonder if he has the necessary resources to respond to intelligent young questioners pointing to the early chapters of the book of Genesis and asking: 'How can you as a science teacher believe this?' He remains convinced – even though he may find it hard to articulate – that science is not fundamentally at odds with religion, but his plea is to know more about the Genesis passages in order to test his own assumptions and to be able to help others have what he would regard as a rounded understanding of both science and religion. And so his question is: 'What does the Bible mean when it says that God created the world?'

This question is not unique to those in Richard's situation. Publicly voiced claims of atheistic scientists are ever more evident and strident. Those who want to salvage anything from the book of Genesis are often cast as ignorant, fundamentalist or just plain stupid. Indeed, they are even seen as part of an irrational religious threat.

> ## TO DO
>
> Do you recognize this questioner's situation? Have you been in a
> similar situation yourself? How have you sought to 'defend' the
> Bible accounts? Have you ever wished to be better resourced?
> How might you frame a question to the Old Testament that
> reflects your experience? Share your answers with other
> members of the group.

The first thing to say is that 'creation' does not only make its biblical
appearance in Genesis. Take the following four examples.

First, in Proverbs 8.22ff. we read an account of creation narrated
by 'wisdom' in the form of a young girl. She is God's darling and
delight (v. 30) and plays around in his creation as a granddaughter
might. She says 'The Lord created me the first of his works' (v. 22).

Second, in the New Testament we read in Colossians 1.16: 'In
him everything in heaven and on earth was created, not only things
visible but also the invisible orders of thrones, sovereignties, authorities, and powers: the whole universe has been created through him
and for him.'

Third, in the familiar passage at the beginning of John's Gospel
we hear that in the beginning was the Word, and that the Word was
with God but subsequently became flesh.

Fourth, Psalm 93.1 is typical of the sentiments of a group of
Psalms (47; 93; 96; 97; 98; 99) that celebrate YHWH's 'enthronement'. They include a complex set of ideas, but central is the claim
that YHWH is the king of creation:

> The Lord has become King, clothed with majesty;
> the Lord is robed, girded with might.
> The earth is established immovably;
> your throne is established from of old;
> from all eternity you are God. (Psalm 93.1–2)

From these four examples we can say that the passages make theological claims to specific contexts. They describe God creating

concepts, such as Wisdom and whatever a Word made flesh might mean. They are also intimately connected with the concept of sovereignty. For example, one contemporary writer sees the claims made in the Enthronement Psalms as amounting to belief in God's victory, and so sovereignty, over the political powers that were faced at the Exodus, his victory over other 'gods', his victory over chaos and his victory over the powers of evil and death (Brueggemann, 2014, p. 49). We can also say that they show that 'creation' language, theology and imagery is capable of a wide variety of applications and reapplications. Clearly these passages were not written by a geologist. 'Creation' is a theological category and not a technical scientific term when it appears in the Bible.

Some of the key passages about creation are found in Genesis 1—11. This section of the book is separate from what follows. From Genesis 12 onwards we read the story of Israel, but the first 11 chapters are more concerned with universal truths, observations and conundrums. There are two things to be said here. The first is that the relation between a universal or even a cosmic God on the one hand, and the particularity of the people of Israel, and individuals within that people on the other, is an ongoing tension throughout the Old Testament. The second is that chapters 1—11 set out questions that they do not answer. The most fundamental of those is perhaps the most basic of all human questions: is it the case that God's grace will ultimately overcome human sin and wickedness; or will human folly inevitably subvert God's goodness (see Clines, 1996)?

TO DO

Think about that last question. Can you list times when you have experienced evil overcoming good, and wondered if there were any point in believing in the power of a good God? On the other hand, can you list times when you have been lifted as good has overcome evil intent? Share your experiences. A consideration of this question is a good way to approach Genesis 1—11.

The history of the study of these chapters takes us through early literal, typological and allegorical studies to more modern times. The nineteenth century marks an important stage. The latter part of that century saw the development of two methods of approach that continued into the twentieth century. The *first* approach was source criticism. This represented an approach to biblical texts similar to that adopted by historical disciplines with regard to other ancient texts. It was part of the attempt to demonstrate that the Bible (and religion in general) was not just for the ignorant, but that it could hold its own in the academy and had nothing to fear from the application of critical method. Source criticism was a way of discovering whether texts were composite; that is, whether they had assumed their present form over a period, from more than one source, or were in fact the work of one hand.

Julius Wellhausen is usually regarded as the pioneer in the field of Old Testament source criticism. (Ironically, his *Prolegomena to the History of Ancient Israel* was published in a series called 'Forgotten Books' in 2008, which in a sense shows its continuing importance – Wellhausen, 1885/2003.) His studies in the Pentateuch – the first five books of the Christian Bible and the first section, the Torah, of the Hebrew Bible – identified four different sources, representing different periods and theological outlooks. A great deal of work has been done since his day to refine further these four different sources and to determine the importance of the theological differences, but essentially his work still stands. He identified the four sources using the letters J, E, D and P. The oldest source was J, using the word Jehovah (YHWH) for God (hence J). It had narrative form and described relations between God and humans in a naïve way (God just wanders about in the Garden of Eden when he wants to speak to Adam, for example – Genesis 3.8).

The E source calls God Elohim (hence E). This describes a greater distance between humankind and God. God now appears in dreams (Genesis 28.12) rather than face to face. This source is a little later than J and comes from a different geographical area. At some stage their two accounts become edited together as JE. The D source is considerably later. The D stands for Deuteronomistic, and this source includes the whole of the book of Deuteronomy. The D writers – as we shall call them – had an agenda that was prompted by the experience of exile. Their writings were an attempt to unravel why this dreadful disaster had overtaken Israel and how a repetition could be avoided. The final writers are known as P. This is meant to stand for Priestly writers since this source has a particular interest in liturgy and ritual. The P might equally well stand for 'publishers' because these were the people who presented the Pentateuch in its final form. They contributed huge new chunks of material, such as the book of Leviticus, and edited the rest, adding new material interweaved with what they received. They too had an agenda and a different view from that of the D writers on how to avoid the disaster of exile.

This last point is important. The Pentateuch does not contain one 'party line', it actually presents a problem and then suggests different ways of responding to it. What this conclusion also reminds us of is that the last editors, the P writers, were the ones to introduce the whole publication with their own preface. Thus it is that Genesis 1, a statement of P theology, is much later in origin than Genesis 2, which is JE. Genesis 2 was written before the Exile. Israel was confident, society was settled, and this account of creation reflects a view of humankind as sovereign within the created order. They are created first – man, then woman. They get to name the animals and so on. Then there is a Fall, an act of disobedience that could be seen as an attempt to usurp the unique role of God, and so a series of checks and balances is put in place that in the process seek to explain the origins of marriage, childbirth and the world of work. Such attempts are known by the technical term 'aetiological'.

By the time of the P writings there is a very different estimate of 'man's inhumanity to man' after the Holocaust of the Exile. There is a new understanding of what would now be called ecological issues and a new sense that a different kind of relationship between humankind and the rest of creation was called for if life on earth were to be sustainable. So in this account in Genesis 1, humans come last into a creation already connected and functioning. They come tentatively as guests who have to learn their place and they come together as male and female. Interestingly (to Richard at least), the order in which creation is described is not unlike that favoured by some evolutionists.

TO DO

Divide the group into two. One subgroup reads Genesis 1.1—2.3, the other reads Genesis 2.4—3.24. Now imagine there is a proposal to build a nuclear reactor in the area. Based on what you have read, each group makes a 'theological response' as part of the local debate. How different are they? What does this suggest to you about the accounts?

The nineteenth century also saw new opportunities for travel and for the development of the archaeology of the holy lands. The effect of this was to learn far more about ancient Near Eastern societies generally and more about religious practice in those societies. This prompted the development of the second approach, the so-called History of Religions School, which found many points of contact between the different religions of the ancient world. So the Bible takes for granted the common assumption of a three-storeyed universe: heaven, earth and the underworld. A passing comparison is possible with creation myths from Babylonian culture but these tend to describe a primordial battle between the gods of order and chaos (Marduk and Tiamat), which is alien to the Old Testament. There are what might be called literary allusions to these myths in some of the Psalms (e.g. 74.13f.; 89.10; 104.7–9). But the attempted application of the myths to the Genesis accounts served only to carry their interpretation further from the world of fact and towards more anthropological or literary interpretations. In the early part of the twentieth century there was something of a revolt caused by these critical methods.

This was not so much a conservative backlash – though of course any kind of biblical criticism produces those – as an anxiety that study of the Old Testament had, first, become a matter of ever more detailed textual source analysis, which missed the bigger picture.

There was some truth in this as source criticism had given way to a *third* approach: form criticism. Form criticism might more appropriately be called transmission analysis, because that is its concern. It asks in what historical context a portion of text might have originated and then tries to trace its subsequent history of transmission until it becomes embedded in the larger text we now have. Form critical studies try to trace that process, starting with the finished text and working backwards. The process demonstrates just how wedded critics of that time were to historical methods of criticism. They felt that the further back towards its origins you traced the history of a text, the more likely it was that you could discover the truth it contained. The method led to conclusions that were often conjectural, and which focused on small sections of text, sometimes at the expense of seeing the bigger context.

But second, there was a sense at the beginning of the twentieth century that the Old Testament had become little more than a door on the corridor marked 'ancient religion', a phenomenon among many with few distinguishing marks. Indeed, there was concern that the specific identity of the Old Testament was being lost; that the link between faith communities and the Old Testament was being lost; that the link between the Old Testament and the New Testament was being lost; that a bigger picture was being overwhelmed by a lot of detail. And so was born the discipline of Old Testament theology, as opposed to Old Testament critical introduction, a distinction also used in New Testament studies.

In fact there had been attempts since the eighteenth century to distinguish between the two approaches, but the project really got under way in the twentieth century with Walther Eichrodt's *Theology of the Old Testament*. Published initially in German, it reached a wider audience later in the century when translated into English (Eichrodt, 1964). Eichrodt attempted to answer the question: 'What is the Old Testament about? What is its theme?' He was writing at a time when systematic theologies were still popular, and so he wanted to describe the Old Testament in terms of a system; to see it as interconnected by a single theme or theological category that controlled its arrangement of ideas.

The concept he came up with, as a result, was that of covenant: the agreement between humankind and God, first cemented at Mount Sinai according to the biblical tradition, and famously including the so-called ten commandments (Exodus 20—24). This appeared to be a sensible suggestion. The idea of covenant does appear in many parts of the Old Testament and is clearly a central theme. However, it is not the only theme; it is not equally distributed, and for our purposes it does not appear at all in Genesis 1—11.

The other great figure of early twentieth-century Old Testament theology is Gerhard von Rad. He echoed the dissatisfaction that had prompted Eichrodt but disagreed with his approach in principle. He did not believe that it was right to 'impose' a system on a work that did not actually have a system. He believed that this approach did not do justice to the dynamic of the Old Testament, which described a God who acts in history. He wanted to 'get inside' the faith world of the Old Testament rather than stand outside it with organizational principles, as he accused Eichrodt of doing. Von Rad did so by identifying early creeds or statements of religious belief, such as Deuteronomy 6.20–24.

TO DO

Read Deuteronomy 26.5–10 and Joshua 24.2–14. These are both statements of the kind that von Rad identified. Now try to get hold of a modern creed or statement of belief (such as the Westminster Confession), or a liturgy such as the Covenant Service of the Methodist Church. What are the similarities and differences between the Bible and these more modern 'creeds'? Imagine yourself as a member of a faith community for which the Bible statements were your main statements of identity. What view of God would you have? How does that differ from the view of God prompted by modern confessions?

For von Rad, the original religion of YHWH saw God as a liberating God: a God who acts in history to save God's people. And so the term 'salvation history' seemed appropriate to describe history as viewed through the eyes of faith in such a God. This study was the parent in many ways of subsequent liberation theologies that played a large part in religious life in some communities in the second half of the twentieth century. Typical sentiments from contemporary writers influenced by von Rad's approach include: 'There is no knowledge of YHWH except through his political activity on behalf of the weak and helpless of the land' (Cone, 1997, p. 65); or 'Again and again it has been a story of struggle from oppression, exploitation and injustice. Again and again the God of the Old Testament is recognized as one who has taken sides in that struggle' (Ceresko, 1992, p. 303).

For Richard's purposes this suggests two things. First, that the Bible, as well as not trying to use geographical methodology, is not trying to use history as we know it either. If we can be talking about accounts in the Old Testament in terms of 'salvation history', that suggests something rather different from history as historians might describe it. Second, if the religion of YHWH began and was controlled by what we might call political theology (that is, the effects of God working within the historical social and political sphere), then placing descriptions of creation at the beginning of the Bible, as if that were the starting point, is rather misleading. Rogerson paraphrases von Rad thus: 'Israel knew its God first as redeemer and only later came to confess that he was Lord of the universe' (Rogerson, 2004, p. 14). What Richard wants to know, therefore, is: 'What prompted this creation thinking?' and 'What place does it have in the Old Testament as a whole?'

There is no one simple answer to this question. While von Rad's view that creation theology was subsequent to liberation theology is widely accepted, some scholars would not agree with him that creation is a late addition, and would want to point to, for example, the Enthronement Psalms and others – such as Psalm 89, which combines liberation and creation motifs – as evidence of a belief that the God who had the power to free and, in a sense, create a people was also sovereign over other forms of chaos and disorder. In other words, as Anderson puts it: 'Contrary to the present arrangement of the biblical drama, the theological movement is not from the confession "God is the Creator" to "Yahweh the God of Israel is the Redeemer," but in just the opposite direction' (Anderson, 1994, p. 26). That points to a potential for creation theology perhaps, rather than the developed presentation, which we find not in Genesis at all but in Isaiah. One of the most accepted results of source criticism is that the book we call Isaiah actually falls into three parts. The part that deals with creation theology is the second part, chapters 40—55. These are the parts that derive from the Exile.

In recent study the Exile has come into far greater prominence than hitherto. Until the last quarter of the twentieth century, scholars in fact paid little attention to it. It is hardly mentioned in the Old Testament, and certainly does not have anything like so high a profile as the Exodus as a determining narrative. A number of factors have changed that. One of them is the realization that it was the Exile that appears to have been the trigger for publication of the Torah, certainly, and for a new era of theological thinking that eventually resulted in the literature we now classify as Wisdom literature – that is, Proverbs, Job and Ecclesiastes, as well as some Apocryphal books – and Apocalyptic writing, which we find in the Old Testament in the second half of the book of Daniel and more widely in inter-testamental writings. What was it about this disaster that was responsible for this theological creativity?

We could argue that, just as in the New Testament with the crucifixion, an event had happened that demanded a complete reassessment of what the faithful felt they knew about God. In the Old Testament context, this was a God who had promised his people a special relationship, a land of their own and progeny in perpetuity. The Exile must have seemed to such people like a series of broken promises, and presumably their faith was shipwrecked by the experience. But our Old Testament is the product of people who continued in faith despite this disaster, on the grounds that it was not God who had failed but rather people had got it wrong about God, and there were new things they needed to learn.

TO DO

Have you ever thought about why the Old Testament was written at all? Bearing in mind what this chapter has already introduced, which of the following do you think are promising leads on the way to an answer:

- To provide a record of the history of Israel?
- To provide some core documents for the faith of Israel?
- To persuade people about the value of faith?
- To encourage people to embrace faith as a means of maintaining peace and harmony in society?

What are the implications of your choices for your understanding of the role of the Bible today?

With regard to those lessons there were two distinct schools of thought. One, represented by the D tradition (Deuteronomists), was that the disaster had been brought about by human sin and neglect of the covenant demands, but that the prime responsibility for this lay with Israel's leaders. Their prescription was adherence to a 'second law'. The other group, P, writing a little later, were less concerned with the question, 'How could God let this happen?' – though they had a view on that – than with asking, 'How can we prevent this happening again?' And their answer was to introduce a new theology that we might, nowadays, call sacramental. Among other things, they felt that the land that had been gifted to the people had been carelessly defiled, and that the careful balances and relationships that characterized harmony in society had been broken, and indeed that the prime relationship between God and humankind had suffered in the process. The P tradition has no story of the Fall such as the one we find in Genesis 3, but it has been argued that for these writers there is nonetheless an awareness of what we might call the Fall. According to a scholar who has made a particular study of the P traditions, three contributory factors to the Fall were human violence, ungratefulness for God's gifts and lack of trust in God (Lohfink, 1994, pp. 99–113). What the P tradition does give us, however, is Genesis 1. In its publication context this can be seen as a corrective, a statement of a new theological perspective, expressed in a semi-liturgical form, which will introduce the later practical implications of P theology.

The contribution of the Exile to creation theology does not stop there, however. One of the theological insights that emerged from the experience of exile was the embrace of monotheism. It is easy to imagine from a reading of the Old Testament that the community of YHWH faith lived in a monotheistic culture; that is, a culture that held that there is just one God. However, it is much more likely that the culture was pluralistic and that the community of YHWH faith was in a competitive relationship with communities following other gods. Narratives such as 1 Kings 18, historic hints in the settlement accounts such as at Judges 3.6 and perceived polemic in liturgies contained in the Psalms (see Brueggemann, 2014, pp. 42, 49), all provide evidence of that. The culture of polytheism clearly had its own rules and was widespread. In 2 Kings 5 a Babylonian, Naaman, is cured of leprosy by the prophet Elisha. He is so grateful that he promises to worship YHWH from now on but he requires two buckets of Hebrew earth to take back to Babylon with him so that he can worship the Hebrew God YHWH on Hebrew soil (2 Kings 5.17).

The Exile changes this perception for the people of Israel. Their prophets Ezekiel and Isaiah speak to them within Babylon. God sees and knows them there. He is not bound by the geographical constraints of Israel. More than that, he is arranging world political affairs so that the current Babylonian powers will be overcome by the Persians at the hands of Cyrus (Isaiah 45.1ff.). This helps a process towards monotheism that may have been gathering momentum before the Exile. God is no longer seen as the best god among many. Now God is the only God, an international God. And that realization leads to others. If God is able to arrange the political affairs of other nations, God must be the God of all history. If God is the only God, God must be the God of all peoples. And prior to both of those, if God is the only God then God, and no other, must be the God of all creation. Each of these realizations leads to new avenues of creative thinking and writing, and that is especially true in the case of the realization that God is the God of all creation.

This realization leads directly to what we call the Wisdom litera-ture. The argument runs like this. If God is the God of all creation and continues to take an interest in creation, then we should be able to learn something of God from the study of creation – to learn about the designer from studying the design, as a much later rationalization might put it. And so we get the book of Proverbs, an exercise in what we might now call social science. By seeing what appears to work well in human intercourse we can learn more about God's plan, and learning more about God's plan leads us to a closer realization about, and relationship with, God. But this is a two-edged sword. Before long, experience demands an answer to the question: 'If God is the sole creator of the world, why does it not work much better, and why should there be suffering and injustice?' The book of Job addresses that situation. We shall look at these works in due course, but for the moment we should note that the most exuberant claims for God as creator come from within the Exile, in the voice of 2 Isaiah (as we shall call the second part of the book), and that that is the situation of theological ferment when the first five books of the Bible were published. Creation theology is not an original dogmatic assertion. It is at least partly a consequence of theological reflection on the experiences of liberation and exile.

When it is taken as a standalone doctrine, creation theology can actually be quite socially dangerous. It can be taken to mean that the status quo is what God intended. This verse of a hymn origin-ally composed to teach children the first article of the creed is now usually omitted:

The rich man in his castle
The poor man at his gate
God made them high and lowly
And ordered their estate.

Hence the injustices of the present can be ignored. Regimes such as apartheid in South Africa can be shored up. Those who have done well, even at the expense of others, can claim God's favour, and so on. Psalm 33 is a good example of what worship means to a congregation who have done well in this life and so completely bought into creation theology. They have done well because they deserved to do well. It was no accident.

TO DO

Read Psalm 37.18–28. What picture springs to your mind of the speaker here? How close is his view to the realities of life? What newspaper would he read?

So we see that the creation accounts in Genesis may not be geographically or scientifically interesting but they are theologically compelling. They illustrate the direction of Old Testament study over a century and indicate some of the most interesting current discussions and debates in the field. Interest now centres on different ways of reading the texts and draws attention to the reader rather than the author.

Reading the texts following the disciplines of historical study still brings results. There continue to be studies in the distinctive theologies of P or D, and theories about how and why the sources were intertwined in the way they are. Readings that use the disciplines of literary study rather than history have become more popular in recent years. Students of literature are less interested in the origins and transmission of text as in the way the text impacts on present experience. Importantly, they believe that the truths texts contain are revealed in the relationship between the text and its present reader. They tend to look at larger portions of text. Liberation readings ask whether there are coded messages in Genesis 2 and 3 that relate to the excesses of Solomon's reign. Feminist readings seek to rebut the misogyny of Genesis 2 and textual critics argue over the correct translation of Genesis 1.28: should humans *shepherd* the earth or *subdue* it, with the very different implications of each translation?

TO DO

Imagine yourself as Richard, getting this response to his question. How satisfied would you be? How might you arrange material for a class of sixth-formers on the theme 'Creation in the Bible and today'?

Did this response answer the question as you framed it for yourself? Does it leave unanswered questions for you or does it prompt you to think afresh about some aspect of God? Share your answers with the group.

Actually Richard was pleased with the answer, so far as it settled his immediate concern, but new questions were raised for him in connection with what the creation accounts were probably saying. These were questions about power and authority, about social mobility and liberation and about what we do in liturgy. One other comment caught his eye as a matter for further thought as he looked up one of the references:

> ... the danger of a retreat from the dimension of the cosmological into the dimension of the anthropological, the existential or the aesthetic is that the realm of the non-human – what we call nature – may come to be regarded as theologically out of bounds. This in turn may foster a sharp dichotomy between religion and science, resulting in an abdication of responsibility for the environment in which we live and move and have our being. Theologians today find themselves in a time of startling new horizons of science – in astronomy, physics, biology, medicine and more – and that calls for a theology with cosmological interests. (Anderson, 1994, p. 99)

What do you think is the right relation between religion and science?

Further reading

Alter, R., 1982, *The Art of Biblical Narrative*, New York: Basic Books.

Brueggemann, W., 1982, *Genesis* (Interpretation Commentaries), Atlanta, GA: John Knox Press.

Gunn, D. M. and Fewell, D. N., 1993, *Narrative in the Hebrew Bible*, Oxford: Oxford University Press.

Holdsworth, J., 2005, *SCM Studyguide to the Old Testament*, London: SCM Press.

Trible, P., 1984, *Texts of Terror*, London: SCM Press.

Wenham, G. J., 2000, *Story as Torah*, Edinburgh: T. & T. Clark.

2

If God really gave the promised land to just one race and helped them get rid of the original inhabitants, does this mean God condones ethnic cleansing?

In Richard's sixth-form is a student called Zoe. Zoe hopes to go to university next year to study international politics. She is particularly interested in the politics of the Middle East, where she lived for a short time while her father was working in the UAE. She is loosely attached to a local church too. She is attracted not so much by the services as by the availability of a really enjoyable Sunday-night teenage discussion group that meets at the home of a young couple in the parish who don't seem to mind having their house invaded once a week. The question that concerns her stems from her study of the Palestinian issue in particular, and the way contemporary religious expressions of Christianity seem to play a role. She is anxious about the idea that God gave people a promised land and that that gives them a right to it over other kinds of claim, and so she frames her question for her discussion group: 'If God really gave the promised land to just one race and helped them get rid of the original inhabitants, does this mean God condones ethnic cleansing?'

The anxieties behind Zoe's question have been shared by scholars in the second half of the twentieth century. That may be partly due, as her version of the question perhaps suggests, to the establishment of the state of Israel in 1948, and the repercussions of that religio-political decision on the region, and especially on the Palestinian people. But that is only part of the reason for scholarly interest. New insights from sociology and archaeology, as well as continued close study of the texts, have also led to a reassessment of the status of those Bible passages that tell of the birth of Israel, of the Exodus, the Conquest and the Settlement. If we might rephrase Zoe's question in a way that corresponds to this scholarly interest, we could ask: 'Can we trust the biblical accounts as a record of what really happened?'

TO DO

Try to get hold of a copy of the film *The Ten Commandments*, and watch it as a group. Does this portrayal of the Old Testament as a definite historical record raise any questions for you? Are they along the same lines as Zoe's question?

Now, as a group, share in turn any conclusion from the book of Genesis that you think is important for the ongoing story of Israel. Check your list against the one below.

First, let us remind ourselves of what the Bible actually says. It is the book of Exodus that actually begins the history of the 'national' religion of YHWH, as a communal enterprise, following the initial writings, axioms and structural manoeuvrings (*prolegomena*) of the book of Genesis. That provided us with the name Israel; it described the Hebrew people as essentially ethnically distinct; it traced their origins to a common ancestor, Jacob (whose name became changed to 'Israel' by God – Genesis 32.28); it prompted in its readers the expectation that promises made by God would be fulfilled in the next phase of the story that was about to begin; it served to locate the last of the patriarchs, Joseph, in Egypt.

In Exodus 1.1—3.15 we are introduced to the concept of a Hebrew population of slaves, descended from the patriarchal family of Jacob who had been renamed Israel. It introduces us also to Moses – an Egyptian-named fugitive from Egypt – and it gives us a name for the God of the patriarchs, YHWH (3.14), which could be seen as a kind of riddle and no real answer to the question. It means, approximately 'I am what I am and I will be what I will be.' In Exodus 5 we find that the crisis of the slaves' treatment is being ramped up and, following a series of plagues, Pharaoh is eventually persuaded to let the Hebrew slaves go, which they do on the so-called Passover night (12.28–42). Then 14.5—15.21 recounts the famous incident of the parting of the sea, together with a victory song. The remainder of the book of Exodus is taken up with events in the Sinai desert, particularly at Mount Sinai, where God delivers to Moses the so-called ten commandments. This basis of what will be called a covenant between God and the people of Israel is received and accepted (19.1—20.17; 24.3–8).

TO DO

Which parts of this story do you think are likely to be 'true' from a modern historical perspective? How did you judge that? Do you view some elements of the story as worth less as a faith resource as a result, and if so, why? Share your answers.

There follows a 40-year sojourn in the wilderness, most of it spent in just one place, Kadesh-barnea (Numbers 10.29–36 and chapters 14 and 21 give a flavour of all this). This is followed by the conquest of Canaan. The people of Israel en masse approach Jericho from across the river in the Transjordan area, and in a great battle, accompanied by signs from YHWH, the great fortress of Jericho is conquered, quickly to be followed by the destruction of Ai. (The main battles are described at Joshua 6—7, 9—10.) The land is then distributed among the 12 tribes of Israel (Joshua 13—23). The people of Israel inhabit the land, victorious against any local tribes that resist them. Their conquest and settlement is complete and effective. This is followed by a gathering of the people at Shechem, convened by Joshua, which reaffirms the Sinai covenant commitments (Joshua 24).

In real history, there is general agreement that the period in which these events were set was the break between the late Bronze Age and the early Iron Age, roughly between 1250 BC and 1025 BC. The breakdown of society that accompanied the end of the Bronze Age in the eastern Mediterranean area has been compared to the end of the Roman Empire in its effects. It led to political chaos, breakdown of economic life with consequent shortages and suffering and mass migrations, particularly from north to south, from Syria and Anatolia towards Egypt. Egyptian reliefs show refugees streaming into Egypt, with Egyptian forces attempting to prevent them, regarding them rightly as a destabilizing force in an already destabilized setting. On another front, 'sea peoples', probably originally from the Aegean area, were taking coastal land from what had been Egyptian control, and were settling the Mediterranean coastal areas around Gaza – the Philistines of the biblical record. Settlers began to live in hitherto sparsely populated areas, including the hill country of Palestine (the Midianites of the Old Testament) and Transjordan (the immediate setting for the story as set out above). That much is accepted by historians, as is its impact. 'As we seek to understand the sudden appearance of the Israelite religious community, we should not underestimate the world-shattering impact this civilization-wide collapse had on those who survived it' (Mendenhall, 2001, p. 45). The questions are, 'What is the relation between this real history and what the Bible says?' and 'What is the best way to discover that?' One way is to look closely at the text itself in the light of modern critical method.

The story of the Exodus confronts the modern reader with the problem of disentangling legend from history. The story contains miraculous elements and obvious literary devices (such as the 40-year sojourn – in the Bible generally, '40' represents a period of vocational discernment). But it also contains conflicting accounts of the route for the journey. The numbers mentioned at Exodus 12.37 are clearly wrong. Also it is clear, from the repetitions and incon-sistencies in the story as a whole, that several traditions have been woven together, and in that situation it is easy to disregard some of the details. For example, it is often taken for granted, as later writers wish to assert, that the people of Israel were an identifiable ethnic group (based on common ancestry) as they left Egypt. Some comments in the text appear to question that. At 12.38 the people who accompanied Moses are said to comprise a 'mixed crowd', and at Numbers 11.4 they are described dismissively as 'a mixed group of strangers'. In fact the question of exactly when the people involved became an identifiable group called Israel, what exactly they had in common, and where exactly they came from, is a hotly disputed subject of contemporary scholarship, which in turn relates to the issue Zoe identified: 'What do we understand by conquest?'

Another possibility is to use the findings and insights of archaeologists. Biblical archaeology is a discipline that has changed hugely in the past one hundred years. The direction of scholarship in the twentieth century could be characterized as follows: at the beginning of the period the Bible accounts were taken as the hard evidence, and archaeology was brought in to try to confirm that; at the end of the century the archaeological findings were taken as the hard evidence and it was left to Bible scholars to adjust their views in the light of it. In any case, there are limits to what this discipline can provide and there is still room for a large measure of interpretation. However, archaeology can find no trace of evidence for the Exodus on any possible route for a journey across the Sinai peninsula, even at Kadesh-barnea, where with a near forty-year settlement one might have expected to find something. In fact the earliest evidence discovered there dates to the tenth century, two hundred years after the accepted date of the Exodus.

Some archaeological data has actually been revised during the last one hundred years. For example, early twentieth-century excavation at Jericho purported to find evidence of the demolished and burned city walls that Joshua 6 describes. Later work in the 1950s using more sophisticated techniques showed that this evidence dated from several hundred years before the date of the Conquest, and that by the time Joshua arrived, the city had been uninhabited for around two hundred years. Also, absolutely no record of any artefact from the period in question has been found in Jericho. Excavations at Ai – described as a great battle site in Joshua 7 – also failed to yield the expected results. The contemporary archaeologist William Dever, following an exhaustive review of all the evidence, or lack of it, from all the sites mentioned in Joshua, concludes: 'We must confront the fact that the external material evidence supports almost nothing of the biblical account of a large-scale, concerted Israelite military invasion of Canaan' (Dever, 2003, p. 71).

TO DO

Read Joshua 6. If this is not a historically accurate account, can you identify details in the story that might give some clues as to why it was written like this? What do the writers want us to believe?

On the basis of earlier work, the early twentieth-century archaeologist and scholar W. F. Albright (1939) believed that the conquest account as set out in the book of Joshua was essentially viable. He was followed in the first half of the twentieth century by a succession of conservative scholars based in the USA. One of Albright's students, John Bright (1960), was responsible for a standard history of Israel on which many current clergy were raised, and which supports his view.

An alternative theory held by a number of German scholars, including Albrecht Alt (see Alt, 1968) and Martin Noth (see Noth, 1960), was developed in the 1920s and 1930s. They were concerned about the historicity of the Conquest accounts and believed that Israel had been formed through a peaceful integration or infiltration that had not involved battles or warfare at all. In fact this theory recalled Israel's nomadic tribal pastoral past and pointed to the modern experience of migrating Bedouin as evidence. The suggestion was that over time these migrants began to settle in the hill country and became the Israelites of later tradition. According to Noth (1960, p. 88), different groups formed a kind of coalition, which he called an amphictyony, drawing on a sixth-century BC Greek model. This theory too has problems. Material evidence, which in fairness it would be hard to imagine, is nonetheless lacking. It is claimed that the traditions describing Israel's pastoral life, on which the theory is largely based, may themselves be fanciful, and the Bedouin do not in fact provide the modern model claimed for them. Later studies have found difficulties with the amphictyony model.

In 1962 George Mendenhall introduced a new theory, based on insights from sociology. His article, 'The Hebrew Conquest of Palestine' (Mendenhall, 1962), claimed that the rise of Israel as an identifiable religious community was not primarily the result of external immigration or aggressive conflict of any kind. It was rather the triumph of the innovative religious ideas of Yahwism that captured imaginations, particularly of the very ethnically and socially diverse existing population, and led to – what he later regretted calling – 'a peasants' revolt' against the oppressive and corrupt powers of Canaan, which in turn led to the formation of a Yahwist religion that took the name Israel. In other words, the 'conquest' was not an external one but an internal one. That raised questions about the biblical claims of ethnic homogeneity made for Israel, and in what could be seen as an extension of Mendenhall's theory (though he has disagreed with some aspects of it), at the close of the 1970s Norman Gottwald (1979) published his magisterial work, *The Tribes of Yahweh*.

This work approached the issues from the standpoint of sociology and from an avowed Marxist background. He agreed with Mendenhall that the 'conquest' actually involved a lengthy period of struggle against Canaanite overlords, and that Israel resulted from those participants in the struggle who took as their inspiration, rather than any ethnic connection, the liberating power of the god YHWH, memory of which had been brought to the area by some escaping slaves. Scholars were initially suspicious of his Marxist credentials, and 'Few appreciated his stress on indigenous origins or his emphasis on ideological and social factors in long-term cultural change. But these insights ... have proven brilliantly correct, even if largely intuitive at the time' (Dever, 2003, p. 54).

TO DO

The picture Mendenhall and Gottwald paint is a breathtaking one, of a society starting from scratch, following disaster and disillusion, with a new experimental understanding of how a religious community can work. Can you think of any modern examples of such a thing? You might think about the following (you may need to do some research):

- The Iona or Corrymeela communities;
- Shaker communities in the USA;
- The Münster experiment by Anabaptists in the sixteenth-century Reformation;
- Cistercian monastic communities in medieval England.

Mendenhall has spelt out more precisely the theological basis of the appeal. He sees this as a new model for community in a context where former models were in shambles. Formerly, communities were bound together either ethnically, by force and coercion or by law. This community would be bound together by commitment to ten basic principles – and that is how Mendenhall understands the theophany at Sinai. 'The only homogeneity that existed among these people was their shared commitment to a very fundamental definition of human integrity – in other words, their basic value system' (Mendenhall, 2001, p. 62). So he speaks of the ten commitments, rather than ten commandments. If these were to be taken as laws (as in fact they have often been understood in Western interpretation), he argues, they would be far more detailed and far less amenable to local cultural interpretation (pp. 63ff.). For him this is the passionate theological heart of the Old Testament. The attempt to preserve and defend the integrity of those commitments, he believes, is the substance of much of the subsequent writing in the Old Testament.

He also drew attention to the way later writers who wanted to adapt the Sinai revelation to their own times were not afraid to revise the Sinai story.

> **TO DO**
>
> Read Exodus 19; 24.9–13 and 34.4–29. These passages describe a whole series of trips up and down the mountain. What explanation can you find for them all? What revisions do you think might have been involved? What does this say about the integrity of the composition of the account as a whole?

Mendenhall paints a picture of disillusioned people wanting to make a fresh start, and dismissing the failed political models of which they had been aware. 'The point is that these hill-country villagers had little use for political power structures, great contempt for the value systems that necessitated them and deep dissatisfaction with the old Bronze Age religious cults that legitimized them' (Mendenhall, 2001, p. 78). He compares these people to the early Christians. Like them, this commitment to YHWH as their leader, their king, meant that they had no prior allegiance to a political figure, a local king, hence the religion was open to 'international' status – all who regarded YHWH as king could be part, and the important thing was that each 'member' was personally bound to YHWH by covenant.

> **TO DO**
>
> Do you think there is a comparison to be made between these YHWH communities of 'Israel' as Mendenhall sees them, and the life of the early Christians? Can you see any link between either of them and the life of faith communities today? Do we have something to learn from them today?

It is interesting in this context to read about the public debate concerning a 'local' king that we see in 1 Samuel 8 and 9. In chapter 8 we see Samuel setting out the case against having a king. YHWH is their king. If they have a local king they will find that they are subject to all the restrictions and bad practices that their forebears had reacted against in adopting the new religion in the first place. They would lose their distinctive identity. They would be just like other nations. But in 8.19f. the people say that they want to turn back to that system. They want to be like other nations. They want to fight wars and adopt a political system once again based on coercion and force. It is part of the D writers' agenda to locate the point at which the people strayed from the covenant ideals.

This voluntary acceptance of a radical new community structure and understanding is a key point for Mendenhall. He points out that the earliest biblical sources of Exodus 15 and Deuteronomy 32 speak of God's *created* people rather than God's *chosen* people. This created people had a different view of war (hence the irony of the last paragraph). Holy war, says Mendenhall, was entirely defensive, fought within the borders of the holy land; that is, the land owned by YHWH. There was no aim for territorial expansion. The institution of the 'ban' meant that no one could profit from the spoils of war (a point emphasized with the story of Achan in Joshua 7.1, 19–26). Those who fought were volunteers not conscripts, and YHWH was the leader.

For Mendenhall (2001, p. 81), supported by what he calls an 'overwhelming number of biblical scholars', the account of the Conquest as described in Joshua 1—11 is 'almost entirely fictitious, created by a much later scribe who could not imagine the early Yahwist federation being all that different from the politically organized imperialistically driven Israel of his own day' (Mendenhall, 2001, p. 92). He represents one way of moving *from* archaeology and accepted 'real' history, *to* the Bible, rather than vice versa. He paints a picture of a coalition or federation of different ethnicities, tribes, clans and social groups in the hill country of Transjordan and Palestine that have in common an allegiance to YHWH – almost as a protest against the systems that have resulted in the former breakdown of civilization – and are committed to ten principles, capable of local and cultural adaptation. This is a Reformation, which later generations, tempted back into old religious practices, misunderstand and misrepresent.

So how does Mendenhall think the 12 tribes were formed, and the YHWH community became located in Palestine and Transjordan? First, he points out that of all the people who left Egypt only two, Joshua and Caleb, actually entered the land (Numbers 14.24; 32.11f.). The rest lived out their lives in either the Sinai or Transjordan hills. He believes that the literary attempts to gloss over this are clumsy and not persuasive. He then sees a two-stage process in which a relatively settled group of the people who left Egypt, now at Kadesh-barnea, were living a peaceful pastoral life there, and moving seasonally with their herds and flocks to pastures, the right to graze being sometimes negotiated with local authorities and warlords. At some point there is a clash between these herdsmen and the tiny fiefdom of Sihon of the Amorites (Numbers 21.21–32), which the Yahwists win. He believes that the inhabitants of that land, glad to be rid of Sihon, make common cause with them, that some are probably refugees or from refugee stock in any case and that they become known as the tribe of Reuben. This is the tribe that the Bible puts first in its lists (e.g. Numbers 26.5), and it makes sense, Mendenhall claims, to think of them as the first formed. That marks the end of the first phase. 'The population [of the Transjordan highlands] comprised villages belonging to the tribes and clans of Reuben, Gad, Machir, and Gilead. A federation was beginning to form' (Mendenhall, 2001, p. 83). The second phase sees a similar gathering movement into Palestine, attracting disaffected former subjects of other petty warlords.

There is a third contributory factor in the new interpretation of these texts, alongside archaeological findings and sociological insight. That is the new popularity of literary criticism. From the 1970s onwards, and mirroring the cultural shift from a modern to a postmodern culture in the West, there has been a growing sense that reading the Old Testament texts using the critical methods employed by historians has revealed all it can. Valuable as its insights have been, they are incomplete. So scholars have begun to read the texts using the tools employed by students of literature, and that has had a profound impact on Old Testament study generally (for examples see Brettler, 1995, pp. 2ff.).

Instead of looking for the 'truth' or 'meaning' of a text in its historical origins, scholars have concentrated rather on the intentions of the writer, the means by which those intentions are accomplished and the response this has elicited in the reader. This approach has found common cause with some aspects of sociological study, particularly that no text is innocent; it is always furthering an interest. That has prompted the so-called hermeneutic of suspicion, in which the question 'Why did the author write thus?' is further refined into the question 'In whose interest did the author write?' (a classic study of which is Clines, 1995). It has also coincided with a new interest by historians in what we actually mean by history or historical truth, which can result in the reductionist 'all history is created' (Brettler, 1995, p. 1).

The key aspect of this development for our purposes, and in response to Zoe's interest, is that the question 'What really happened?' is becoming less important in discerning meaning and truth. To interpret the Conquest and settlement accounts is therefore to ask a different set of questions:

- What did the assumed writer intend?
- Who was the assumed reader?
- What means of persuasion (rhetoric) was employed to convince the reader?
- What element of character or plot led the reader to a particular conclusion?
- What narrative skills were involved?
- Since the reader is so key, is there a difference between the meaning of these passages for fifth-century BC readers and readers today?

TO DO

Read 2 Samuel 11.1—12.25. What is your estimate of this as part of a serious history? What kind of writing does it most remind you of? What is the effect of this way of presenting the material on you as a reader? Does asking these questions help you to look at the Conquest stories in Joshua 1—11 in a new way?

The movement away from a dependence on the historical accuracy of the biblical accounts is based, then, on a variety of concerns. There is the overriding moral concern, identified by Zoe, and there is the concern about evidence mentioned by all recent writers, relying on the work of a new breed of biblical archaeologists such as Dever and Fritz (see Fritz, 1994). And there is also concern that the textual evidence that describes the conquest and settlement is in some way suspect. Carol Meyers draws attention to the inconsistencies between the major narrative of a 'clean sweep' victory and settlement, and the textual record of Judges 1—2 and elsewhere in the book, which speaks of something far more piecemeal and incomplete. She also points to the lack of any record in the annals of neighbouring peoples about these supposedly earth-shattering events (Perdue, 2001, p. 63). These all coincide with a new interest in literary approaches to the Old Testament and a new awareness of the ideological and rhetorical nature of some of the writing. 'They are highly selective and imaginatively expanded accounts of the meaning and nature of past times. That is, the texts themselves have strong ideological biases that distort or mask events and characters' (Perdue, 2001, p. 67).

Dever, Mendenhall – and those he calls to his support – have in common that they believe the biblical texts derive from a variety of sources, some of which are ancient. From the 1990s onwards, however, there has been a school of thought that, while dismissing the historicity of the Conquest as described in Joshua, does not believe any of the sources to be either ancient or reliable. Rather they take the view that 'Ancient Israel' is a literary construct – or in other words, a historical fiction – designed after the Exile to give legitimacy and a narrative of identity to the post-exile Jews. Philip Davies (1992) is normally credited with introducing this idea. He distinguished between historical Israel (the world to which material artefacts bear witness) and biblical Israel (the sequence of events as recounted in the Old Testament), and concludes that much confusion has been caused by the creation of what he calls 'ancient Israel', namely the attempt to read biblical Israel as if it were historical Israel. His thesis is not confined to the historical books. He believes

Old Testament prophecy also to be a series of late compositions by government-sponsored scribes (Davies, 1992, pp. 117–20).

The title of Keith Whitelam's 1996 contribution to this debate, *The Invention of Ancient Israel*, betrays its content; and its subtitle, *The Silencing of Palestinian History*, pre-empts a great deal of the argument in the book. For him the central concern is: 'the problem that contemporary struggles for land and national identity between Israel and the Palestinians remain unspoken in biblical studies' (Whitelam, 1996, p. 221). Whitelam's view is that scholars such as Noth, Alt, Mendenhall or Gottwald are conditioned by their relationship with the emerging state of Israel and that their horizons are consequently limited. While he accepts that Israel emerged indigenously rather than externally, he objects to the emphasis on 'Israel': 'the prior conclusion that the inhabitants of these sites [i.e. the hill sites in Palestine] are 'Israelite' is not determined from a reading of the archaeological evidence but from a controlling assumption drawn from the Hebrew Bible' (Whitelam, 1996, p. 178).

In the face of these criticisms there has been a number of attempts to claim the ancient origins of sources for the Joshua and Judges texts. Carol Meyers (2001) points to the names of the 12 non-Israelites in Joshua. These have been compared with extra-biblical sources where all 12 are attested as being used in the late Bronze Age period. William Dever's *What Did the Biblical Writers Know and When Did They Know it?* responds to his own question: 'They knew a lot and they knew it early' (Dever, 2001, p. 273). His detailed rebuttal deals not only with archaeological evidence per se but asks questions that he claims have not been faced, about, for example, literary production, the use of oral tradition and what a Hebrew Bible might look like if it had in fact been produced in the Hellenistic period, as Davies and others claim (Dever, 2001, pp. 275ff.).

Zoe's response to this answer is a mixture of relief and anxiety: relief that she is not invited to believe in a ruthless bloody God, but anxiety about the dependability of the biblical text. If nothing is what it seems, how can we read it with any intelligence, she asks. She is trying to come to terms with Carol Meyers's summary about the biblical traditions: 'they can be viewed as a mixture of fictional imagination and historical memory brought together for ideological purposes' (Meyers, 2001, p. 67). What does that mean for the contemporary competing land claims in the Middle East, she wonders.

TO DO

This chapter has introduced some very challenging ideas; for example:

- That what looks like a historical account may be fictional;
- That a huge part of the Bible tradition, based on the Exodus, may have no basis in fact;
- That some scholars think the Old Testament was created to further the interests of a post-exile Judah elite (while others hotly contest that);
- That all the modern political repercussions of a chosen people for a promised land may have no basis in fact.

What is your response to these challenges?

Alongside these challenges, this chapter has also introduced some new 'realistic' pictures of the birth of an exciting alternative religious society or fellowship, reminiscent of some of the beginnings of the New Testament Church. Considering Zoe's initial anxiety, where does it leave you in the interpretation of these texts?

Further reading

Barton, J., 1997, *Making the Christian Bible*, London: Darton, Longman & Todd.

Biggar, S. (ed.), 1989, *Creating the Old Testament: The Emergence of the Hebrew Bible*, Oxford: Blackwell.

Day, J. (ed.), 2004, *In Search of Pre-Exilic Israel*, London: T. & T. Clark.

Fritz, V., 1994, *An Introduction to Biblical Archaeology*, Sheffield: Sheffield Academic Press.

Gooder, P., 2000, *The Pentateuch: A Story of Beginnings*, London: Continuum.

Lemche, N. P., 1998, *The Israelites in History and Tradition*, London: SPCK.

Mills, M., 1999, *Historical Israel: Biblical Israel: Studying Joshua to 2 Kings*, London: Cassell.

3

Is it fair to say that the Old Testament sees no distinction between religion and politics?

Trevor has just celebrated his seventieth birthday. In his formative years in the 1960s he joined the Church as his own protest against the ills of society as he saw them, and subsequently chaired a Justice and Peace group there. During times when the Church was very much identified with social issues, such as the fight against apartheid, the plight of inner cities or the opposition to nuclear weapons, Trevor's faith was nourished by the Old Testament prophets, readings from which were a regular feature of Justice and Peace meetings. Nowadays he sees the Church as having rather turned away from all that, towards something more individual and introspective, which he regrets. His question is really a call for reassurance: 'Is it fair to say that the Old Testament sees no distinction between religion and politics?'

Our studies so far have certainly connected religion and politics. Von Rad's contention that YHWH was first known as a liberator God, freeing people from an oppressive regime, is inherently political. Those Enthronement Psalms that speak of YHWH as king have, according to Brueggemann, a strong polemic intent. If YHWH is king then any earthly king is subordinate to YHWH. That is also a political claim. Even Mendenhall's vision of an intentional religious community, as an alternative to accepted political models, could be said to be making a political point. And the basis of that community's self-understanding, namely the covenant agreement, contains elements such as justice and mercy that are almost bound to have political consequences. It is clear that the more societal and communal the understanding of religion is, the more likely it is to have political consequences. The more individualistic it is, the greater is the likelihood of a divorce between religion and politics. Since our study to date has concerned a political entity drawn together on religious grounds, it is no wonder that it is difficult to separate religion and politics. However, the relation between them is not straightforward or obvious.

TO DO

What dangers do you see in Trevor's approach to the text? Is it right to read the text with a view to having a political perspective ratified, do you think? Can you think of examples on either side of the argument?

Two recent authors make this point as they attempt to find a 'handle' with which to interpret and organize the Old Testament material. Both opt for a bipolar approach. Brueggemann's search is prompted by an attempt to find a new direction for Old Testament study. 'The comprehensive designs of Walther Eichrodt and Gerhard von Rad are now found wanting and we must find a new shape' (Brueggemann, 1992, p. 1). On the one hand, he says, the Old Testament describes a society not unlike that of its neighbours in the ancient world, in that it is recognized as important to have structure and authority for the working of society. Part of the role of religion, he says, is to legitimize that structure. On the other hand, those structures can be oppressive to some, and so a function of the Old Testament is also to draw attention to those on the margins of society in what he describes as 'the embrace of pain'. The tension between the two is the distinctive feature of the Old Testament.

The practice of pain-embrace must always be in tension with the legitimation of structure, never in place of it. It is this tension that is the stuff of biblical faith and it is the stuff of human experience;

... the tension must be kept alive and visible. (Brueggemann, 1992, p. 26)

Rex Mason (1997) makes a similar point in his book *Propaganda and Subversion in the Old Testament*. As that title suggests, he also finds establishment propaganda in the Old Testament, but along-side that is a healthy strain of subversive, even satirical, undermining of that very same establishment. Propaganda can present the claims either of the royal establishment or of the priestly establishment. An example of royal propaganda would be the description of the Covenant made with the house of David in 2 Samuel 7. In its Sinai formulations in Deuteronomy, Exodus and Joshua, the Covenant shows a direct link between God and God's people. Mendenhall regards this relationship as a special characteristic of the first YHWH community. But in 2 Samuel 7 the Covenant is between God and a new establishment entity, the house of David, in perpetuity. It is, unlike the other formulations, without conditions. No matter what David does, from now on God will speak through him. Mason also describes priestly propaganda. Looking at the exclusive claims made for Zadokite priests in Ezekiel 44.10 and 44.15, he traces a gradual move towards those rights and privileges from a situation in which a much larger constituency were regarded as legitimate in their priestly acts (Mason, 1997, pp. 58f.).

The constitutional issues around the appointment of a king provide another interesting example. Deuteronomy 17.14–20 describes the king as a fellow Israelite, subject to the law as everyone else is. Additionally, that law is mediated to the king through the priests and the Levites. His study of the law is to be a kind of discipline. He is, if you like, carrying the burden of being the servant of the servants. He is not described as 'son of God' or in any terms that presuppose he is God's representative on earth. But by the time of Solomon, that concept of kingship has been superseded by a very different one: 1 Kings 10 describes how Solomon receives the seal of approval from 'A-list' celebrity the Queen of Sheba, and goes on to describe Solomon's incredible wealth and power. Bearing in mind that the authors here are the same ones who were responsible for

1 Samuel 8, with its terrible warnings about how kings would be corrupted and would corrupt YHWH religion, 1 Kings 10 stands as a sober description of a worst nightmare come true. Yet the writing is couched in the deep irony of extreme flattery. What we are seeing is the subtle imposition of the D writers' relentless agenda, that the Exile was the fault of bad kings who led their people away from covenant demands.

TO DO

Read Judges 9.7–15. This is the so-called parable of Jotham. It describes how the trees get together to decide to have a king. Those who are capable of doing anything useful are approached but refuse – they are too busy doing their useful things. So in the end the totally useless bramble is made king. What do you make of this story, in the light of our discussion? Can you think of any modern application for it?

The section of the Old Testament of most interest in relation to Trevor's question is that which the Hebrew Bible calls 'Prophets'. This is the second section of the Hebrew Bible, where it is divided there into the Former Prophets and the Latter Prophets. The Former Prophets section contains the books we might think of as history and which, following Martin Noth (for a summary of whose theory and its developments, see Brueggemann, 2003, p. 104), we have described as the Deuteronomistic History, from Joshua through to 2 Kings. It is possible to trace the early development of Old Testament prophecy through those books, though that does not seem to be their main purpose. The Latter Prophets include the writing prophets, some of whom have very long works ascribed to them, such as Ezekiel or Jeremiah, together with a collection of 12 books that probably circulated as a collection in its own right. All those books are quite short, though in some cases nevertheless important.

The earliest prophets of YHWH appear to have emerged in a culture that was content to see a wide variety of different kinds of figure take the name 'prophet'. Some groups of prophets were associated with religious and cultic centres such as Shiloh (1 Samuel 10.5–13; 1 Kings 13.11). These are people sometimes approached by those who have a problem or who want a definitive answer. They act as consultants, sometimes requiring a fee (Numbers 22.7) and sometimes needing a stimulant to be able to function (2 Kings 3.15, but see also Isaiah 28.7). Sometimes prophets are the arbiters of a kind of heads or tails answer to a question (1 Samuel 14.41f.). They are treated as slightly different from the norm of people (2 Kings 9.11, where the prophet is described dismissively as a raving lunatic).

TO DO

Read 1 Samuel 19.19–24. If this were the only record of early prophecy that you had, how would you describe it? Now read Jeremiah 23. How do you think early prophecy differed from its more developed later form?

Kings appear to have had groups of prophets as part of their court retinue. These were people who could be consulted for advice about whether it was a good idea to go to war on a particular occasion, for example. Like sanctuary prophets, court prophets normally operated as a group and, from the Old Testament evidence, appear to tell the king what he wants to hear. Ostensibly all prophets refer to a god (1 Kings 19.18). The Old Testament is at pains to show that true prophets of YHWH are to be distinguished from the false prophets either of other gods, or those who make false claims to be prophets of YHWH: 1 Kings 18.17–40 describes a showdown between the prophets of Baal and the lone prophet of YHWH, Elijah, whom Ahab greets as 'troubler of Israel' (v. 17); 1 Kings 22 describes a showdown between the court prophets and a prophet named Micaiah. All claim to be delivering the authentic word of YHWH. The kings of Israel and Judah want to wage war against the king of Aram. The court prophets are summoned, and in the manner of a latter-day request from a referee to a television judge in a rugby match, the kings ask: shall I attack Ramoth-Gilead or not? (22.6). The court prophets say, yes, and victory will be yours. However Micaiah, who is described as having stood in the councils of YHWH (one of the descriptions favoured by the mainstream prophets), gives a different view, which turns out to be correct, but not before he has been thrown into prison for his pains.

Classic descriptions of speaking truth to power include Elijah's judgement on Ahab in the matter of Naboth's vineyard (1 Kings 21.17ff.) and Nathan's denouncing of David for having committed adultery with Bathsheba (2 Samuel 12.1ff.). In the latter case Nathan employs a clever ruse by which David effectively condemns himself. He tells a story about an obvious violation concerning the lamb of a poor man, which is taken by a rich man. He invites David to judgement. David was very angry about the man in the story (2 Samuel 12.5). Nathan is then able to say, 'You are the man!' (2 Samuel 12.7).

Mason sees this same device being used by later prophets who want Israel to recognize their faults. Several of the writing prophets include 'oracles against the nations', denouncing Israel's neighbours for their wrongdoing (e.g. Isaiah 13—23; Jeremiah 46—51; Ezekiel 25—32). Nahum is, in its entirety, an oracle against other nations, and there are smaller sections in some of the shorter books (e.g. Zephaniah 2.4–15). Mason believes that these are there to lull readers into taking a moral stance that can then be turned against them by confronting them with the sins of Israel. Taking the example of Amos, he believes that 'Amos's hearers would have welcomed and been assured by a series of oracles denouncing their feared and hated neighbours' (Mason, 1997, p. 104). However, exactly the same formula that Amos uses to introduce these oracles is then employed to introduce condemnation of Israel (Amos 1.6—2.3; cf. Amos 2.4–8). This is an example of what Mason calls the subversion – as opposed to propaganda – of the prophets.

The Latter Prophets also denounce false prophets, because authenticity is always an issue when bad news is being delivered. True prophets, on the other hand, usually exhibit a degree of reluctance in being prophets. This is a vocation, not something generally

viewed as a career opportunity. They usually work alone. They need
no stimulants. They take no money. They do not act as consultants.
They claim to have stood in the very court of YHWH and to be
delivering YHWH's word for a particular time and place. This is a
claim with lots of repercussions in terms of power brokering, which
sometimes appears to bring prophets into conflict with priests,
whose role is to safeguard the word of YHWH as a historical inherit-
ance, through tradition.

TO DO

So far we have described the Old Testament prophets as if
they were all men. However, there are mentions in the text of
YHWH prophets who are women. You might like to read Exodus
15.1 (Miriam), Judges 4.5 (Deborah), Isaiah 8.3 (unnamed),
Nehemiah 6.14 (Noadiah) and 2 Kings 22.14ff. (Huldah), the
only one with oracles credited to her. Reading these passages,
do they present any different characteristics of prophecy from
those we have seen in men? Is it of significance, do you think,
that two of the women sing songs? Have we underestimated
the importance of Huldah in the 'discovery' and interpretation
of the scroll that is the basis of the D theology?

All the books contained in the Latter Prophets section could be
described as political, in that they deliver a word to society, usually about changes that need to be made both in attitudes and in
the structural ways societies operate. There is a real correspondence
between the message of those prophets who lived in the eighth and
seventh centuries BC, and the D writers. Those writers, attempting
to find a reason for the punishment of exile, believed that Israel
had brought this disaster upon itself because of its carelessness with
regard to the demands of the Covenant and because of poor political leadership. The prophets in question appear to provide evidence
for that claim, with two hundred years of preaching that the people
and the rulers must change if they wish to avert disaster.

It has been usual to read the books of the Latter Prophets at face value; that is, to read them as if they contain oracles from the periods in which they claim to operate, delivered by the men whose names the books bear. As was once the case with the Gospels, scholars have believed that the biography of the authors could be a means of interpretation (e.g. Heaton, 1996, pp. 14f., 81). This is less usually the case now, and readers are being urged – as part of the more general move to use the tools of literary criticism – to concentrate on the texts themselves rather than a supposed formational history. The period when historical methods were paramount has, though, left us useful insights. There has been a tendency among more conservative scholars, for example, to understand the role of the prophets as being mostly predictive, looking forward to the time of the Messiah, and indeed church lectionaries have contributed to this sense that the most important bits of the Old Testament are the ones that point to the New Testament. In the view of some this has skewed scholarship and left prophetic books that do not have messianic oracles as relatively unknown poor relations from a Christian perspective (e.g. Prévost, 1996, pp. 24f., on Amos). The historical critics have relocated the prophets as people of their own time, speaking to their own situations, however later communities of faith reapplied their words.

In the 1970s and 1980s there was a reaction to the received view that the Old Testament texts should be read as having their own integrity within the Hebrew Scriptures. Rather, they should be read in the light of the use Christian theology has made of them. This 'canonical criticism' appeared to offer a fresh way ahead at the time, and was associated primarily with the American scholar Brevard S. Childs. He believed that 'much of the confusion in the history of Old Testament theology derives from the reluctance to recognise that it is a Christian enterprise' (Childs, 1985, p. 8). This approach has not gained momentum and has attracted significant criticism (e.g. Barr, 1999, pp. 401ff., who describes Childs' isolation within the academic community).

A note of caution is expressed by David Clines in an essay on 'Metacommentating Amos' (Clines, 1995, pp. 76ff.). His title is meant to describe a survey of the presuppositions commentators on Amos employ. His general approach is to use a hermeneutic of suspicion and not to take any text at face value. He believes commentators have been too ready to accept Amos's self-description and motivation. Referring to his attack on the wealthy women (Amos 4.1ff.), Clines wonders whether in fact he might just feel jealous of them, and as to his call from God, that could be simply a way of describing his own determination. While this approach has been taken seriously by some scholars (e.g. Mason, 1997, pp. 129f.), his attempt to question, comprehensively, the conventions of religious writing (e.g. what does it mean to say God 'speaks' to anyone?) have been less popular. It may be, ironically, that another feature of the literary analysis he champions is responsible for that, namely eisegesis. Exegesis is the process of reading a meaning *out* (literally) of a text in the belief that the text 'contains' one meaning, conferred in its origins. This is central to historic modes of criticism. Eisegesis is the reading *into* a text from the reader's experience, in the attempt to find resources for determining truth, which is a feature of literary criticism. Experiences such as 'call' or 'listening to God' can be understood crudely and mechanically but they can also be attempts to articulate something truly experienced by people of faith and recognized by them in the texts without need for 'explanation'; in other words, as a literary convention. Certainly, though, scholars should beware of the possibility of circular argument and the danger of believing that Amos's society was in fact how he describes it, when he may be the only person who sees it like that or may be speaking on behalf of an unrepresentative minority. The awareness of possible 'agendas' is also something always to be kept in mind.

TO DO

Think about the way memorable speech can be reapplied to situations far removed from the original context. Wartime speeches by Winston Churchill might provide examples. How are his phrases made to apply to other situations? Does this shed any light on how traditions develop, or the relative importance of the original context?

Books about this part of the Old Testament tend to distinguish between prophets according to the period in which they 'worked'. They have been taken as the authentic voice of true religion and read against what is known of the true history of the periods in question. While that method still predominates, there is more caution nowadays than there was a hundred years ago about some of its presuppositions. There is less readiness to see the prophets as the spokesmen for religion in their times – their voice, if we are hearing it at all, may have been a minority one. There is more literary caution about whether the contents of the books all derive from the same period or whether, alternatively, the process of collecting oracles was more chaotic than that. Newer forms of criticism have taken a more suspicious view of the prophets than that with which we are presented. Their rhetoric has been noted, and the fact that they appear to have a very close relationship with the D writings and outlook. Of course, all this could be historically genuine but it could also be the case that D editors have reworked some of the material to suit their own case. Nonetheless, at the very least, in answer to Trevor's question, we have to say that the material certainly gives religion a societal and political focus.

TO DO

From any OT Introduction or from a reliable internet site, draw up a timeline history of the period 965 BC–537 BC. Comparison of sites or books will reveal a great deal of agreement. The year 965 marks the approximate accession of Solomon to the throne; 537 is the beginning of the permission for exiles in Babylon to return. Then, using the same sources, mark off the latter prophets against their presumed historical times. In 922 the united kingdom of Israel, which David and Solomon had reigned over, was divided into two. Only two of the prophets operate in the north: Hosea and Amos, both presumed eighth century. Mark off the rest as best you can (dividing the book of Isaiah into three) and then use your scheme as a reference in the rest of the chapter.

As an overall scheme, and dealing only with the most important prophets, Amos, Hosea, Micah and Isaiah of Jerusalem (parts of Isaiah 1—39) are eighth century, prophesying in times of relative historic calm, in the early part of the period at least; with a growing tension towards the end of the century when it seemed that the Assyrian commander Sennacherib might conquer Jerusalem (in 701 BC). Zephaniah, Nahum, Habakkuk and Jeremiah, prophets of the seventh century, were far more conscious of the gathering political crisis for Judah but take different approaches to it. The prophets of the Exile are 2 Isaiah (40—55) and Ezekiel, while 3 Isaiah (56—66), Haggai and Zechariah/Malachi are post-exilic, and dealing with the problems of the return and the reinvention of what was to become Judaism. The eighth-century prophets accuse the state of poor leadership that is allowing or even prompting the people to forget the demands of the covenant relationship with God. These are the writers Trevor so admires, not afraid to speak truth to power.

Jeremiah is the most important of the seventh-century prophets. He is also important in that his autobiography is part of the story against which the book has to be read. Habakkuk and Nahum have different responses to those who are gathering to conquer Israel. Nahum denounces them; Habakkuk is more reflective and asks what God wants us to take from the fact that he is allowing this to happen at all. Zephaniah is more akin to the eighth-century writers.

The prophets of the Exile take very different views and contain the kind of innovative theology that comes from having to come to terms with a disaster like the Exile, in which a completely new estimate of God is called for. The Bible's greatest apologist for creation theology is 2 Isaiah, as we have noted. Ezekiel takes a line recognizable in the P writers as he looks forward to imagine what the new Israel will look like and how it might survive, with a new sense of holiness at its heart. The post-exilic prophets are very bound up with the Temple and Jerusalem as the main symbols of YHWH religion as now understood.

Two books in the collection of the twelve are not really prophetic in the sense that the others are. One is Jonah, which is basically a work of fiction, reflecting on one of the consequences of monotheism: if there is only one God, this God must be the God of all peoples, and God's justice and mercy is not therefore particular but universal. The other is Daniel, the last of the Old Testament books to be written (around 163 BC). Its name means God's judgement, and it is part narrative, telling the story of how Jews fare in the Diaspora, comparable perhaps with the book of Esther, and part vision of a new age – about which more anon.

There is scholarly discussion about the relationship between the Prophets and the Torah, the first two sections of the Hebrew Bible. Brueggemann (2003), while believing that 'there is no doubt that the Torah constitutes the normative canon of Judaism. All else that follows is derivative and of lesser authority' (p. 101), nevertheless concedes that, 'the earliest articulation of what became the canonical faith of the Torah may have been first accomplished by the prophets' (p. 102). In other words, the relationship is more complex than is obvious immediately to the reader. The D tradition of the Old Testament, in seeking to find a way of understanding God's purposes after the Exile, sees the problem as being the disobedience of the people and the decline of respect for, and understanding of, the role of religion in public life. The D movement's prescription of a whole new education programme based on the home, and a new concentration on excellence in religious worship and cultic life by establishing just one centre in Jerusalem, echoes much of what we read in the eighth- and seventh-century prophets.

The link is particularly evident in the book of Jeremiah – one prophet for whom autobiography is a useful critical tool. His father had been a priest at one of the country shrines shut down by the D movement when they had the backing of King Josiah, a king the D tradition takes as its yardstick of authentic kingship (2 Kings 22.2). Jeremiah was an enthusiastic supporter of this movement – a decision that cut him off from his family and gives some insight into the miserable series of introspective 'video diaries' that pepper the book (e.g. Jeremiah 11.18–23; 12.1–6; 15.10–12; 20.7–11). Jeremiah's speaking truth to power consists in confronting people who are in denial about political realities, but also confronting a religious establishment that has colluded with that. Jeremiah 7, an oracle delivered outside the doors of the Temple, and quoted by Jesus, condemns what religion has become, uses the language of idolatry to highlight that and accuses the people more generally of straying from the true demands of the Covenant.

Ezekiel, on the other hand, is written from a temple context that finds echoes in the P strand of the Torah. Recent work on Isaiah has urged against splitting the book into three separate sections, preferring the method of seeing a developing and unified particular tradition and reading the book as a canonical whole (i.e. *as* a book), possibly presenting a third theological option, alongside that of D and P, for the future, based more on the concept of a restored Jerusalem (Brueggemann, 2003, pp. 159, 175). Brueggemann summarizes the state of the question thus:

> it is clear that the literature of the prophetic canon, in very different circumstances and in very different modes, seeks to do in parallel fashion what the Torah seeks to do, namely, to imagine articulate, and evoke a world ordered by and responsive to YHWH,

the creator of heaven and earth and the Lord of Israel's covenant. (Brueggemann, 2003, p. 102)

TO DO

As preparation for the next section, which deals with eighth-century prophets, read Amos 5.21—6.7 and write down what you find as the main themes there.

The book that 'sets the tone' for the judgemental voice of the prophets is Amos, whose importance, according to Brueggemann, 'it is impossible to overestimate' (2003, p. 223). This is the second of the collection of 12 prophetic books and is located in the eighth century. It follows Hosea, which also has notable characteristics. Hosea is written by someone from the north and is directed towards the north. Following the custom of prophetic enactment, in which in some way a prophet's words are given symbolic representation, Hosea's is the most profound example in that he is asked by God to marry a prostitute. The relation between them is turbulent and full of human interest. Whether this is truly autobiographical or simply portrayed as such does not really matter. The image of a deep loving relationship is familiar throughout the prophets section of the Old Testament to describe the relationship between YHWH and YHWH's people. Their carelessness with regard to the covenant relationship can thus be described as the people's adultery or, in more crude terms, whoring. The prophet Ezekiel gives this its most base interpretation and coarse description (chapter 23 is completely given to a detailed allegory along these lines; verse 20 is typical: 'she was infatuated with their male prostitutes, whose members were like those of donkeys, and whose seed came in floods like that of stallions'). Hosea uses this image in a more gentle way, appealing to the feelings of betrayal he has, but how his love overcomes them, making comparison with God's love.

Amos is portrayed as being from the south but delivering his oracles against the north. Again this is possibly less relevant than it seems, because the likelihood is that the book was edited, perhaps after the fall of Samaria in 721 BC, when it was preserved in the south, and that may explain reference to Judah at 2.14f. But the point is more universal than detailed application to Samaria or Judah. That is precisely why Trevor read it in the first place. He could recognize, in what the book condemns, elements of his own society with which he was dissatisfied; and the prescription for the ills it describes is one he believes is relevant in his own situation. The section contained in chapters 3—6 repeats the claims for justice and righteousness (5.7, 24; 6.12) in the face of a society that sees no obvious link between morality and religion, or between public life and religion. It is the contention of the book that such a society is not sustainable and that religion relegated to an entirely private or empty ceremonial sphere is not sustainable either.

The charges in detail are that the people care nothing for straight dealing but 'hoard in their palaces the gains of violence and plundering' (3.10). This is clearly hyperbole. Amos is set in a time of peace, but the book takes a stand on the side of the poor and expresses its theological commentary and testimony from their perspective, or rather that of the God who is on their side. In a similar vein some commentators, from a theological perspective, describe the pain and brokenness and overt violence of the contemporary USA, which would be unrecognizable to many people who live there (e.g. 'Behind the wealth and power of the United States hide despair and a violent culture of denial that drains our humanity' (O'Connor, 2003, p. 5). The indolent wives of the wealthy receive special condemnation (4.1ff.) in words that might seem rather embarrassing to those of us who have become used to even-handed treatment of the sexes. But the political masters are also accused, 'you bully the innocent, extort ransoms, and in court push the destitute out of the way' (5.12). The religious life of the people is mocked. Amos 8.4–7 describes a society where religion has just become a commercial inconvenience and has lost any power to change or direct, and that is what Amos wants to restore. His oracles against the nations, with which he hopes his audience will identify, are a means to bring home to them their own faults. A Day of the Lord is coming. God is not just a dead metaphor but rather a living judge. In what looks very much like a prophecy after the event, the Exile is foretold as the end of all this (7.17).

Amos's message is at one with the D theologians and the religio-political movement they began under Josiah. Society cannot 'inherit the land' and cannot 'rejoice with gratitude', as Deuteronomy might put it, unless it acknowledges society as a gift from YHWH to which it must respond. Religion has to be taken seriously as a moral force and a constant reminder of God's power, at the heart of society. For the D theologians, religion and politics have a symbiotic relationship.

TO DO

Is Trevor right to be happy with this answer? Who do you think is the most important audience in the prophetic oracles? Does later Christian tradition do anything to nullify or moderate what we read in Amos? What do you think are the alternatives to his message? How do you think they compare with New Testament insights as a guide to being the Church in the world?

It would, of course, be wrong to describe the prophets just as political activists using religious language. Their power derives from the direct word that YHWH issues to particular situations, of which they are agents. Their concern is political because God maintains his interest in the world.

Further reading

Brueggemann, W., 1998, *A Commentary on Jeremiah*, Cambridge: Eerdmans.

Carroll, R. P., 1979, *When Prophecy Failed: Reactions and Responses to Failure in the Old Testament Prophetic Traditions*, London: SCM Press.

Davidson, R., 1983, *The Courage to Doubt: Exploring an Old Testament Theme*, London: SCM Press.

Davis, E. F., 2014, *Biblical Prophecy: Perspectives for Christian Theology, Discipleship and Ministry*, Louisville, KY: Westminster John Knox Press.

Mason, R., 1997, *Propaganda and Subversion in the Old Testament*, London: SPCK.

Mills, M. E., 1998, *Images of God in the Old Testament*, London: Cassell.

Prévost, J-P., 1996, *How to Read the Prophets*, London: SCM Press.

Snaith, N. H. (1944) 1997, *The Distinctive Ideas of the Old Testament*, Carlisle: Paternoster Press.

4

How does the Old Testament prophesy the end of the world?

Vi always reads her horoscope. She sees no conflict between this and her lifelong Christian belief. That is partly due to the fact that 60 years ago, when Vi was old enough to take notice of what the preacher at her small chapel was saying, she picked up that God had predestined everyone for particular paths. For her, Christianity was determinist. It said that there was a plan for the future, and a plan for each individual believer within it; a kind of holy horoscope. The parts of the Bible that have always fascinated her most are the book of Revelation and the Old Testament prophets. She has wished above all that she could unlock their secrets, learn their code and be privy to what they point to. She has a particular question, born of the language she has seen in those Old Testament books, which speaks of the future in terms of new kingdoms, new ages and new hopes: 'How does the Bible prophesy the end of the world?'

There are several ways for a learning church community to organize a response to that question. One would be to look at specific prophetic books to explore two issues. The first issue is to see how possible it is to disentangle their forth-telling from the foretelling; that is, to disentangle the commentary contemporary with their own time from future prediction. The second issue is to see how the earliest Christian community used those same books as part of their apologetic about Jesus, following their belief that prophetic foretelling focused chiefly on him. A second approach might be to undertake a thematic study of Old Testament eschatology. This is a technical term derived from the Greek word *eschata*, meaning 'last things'. In the middle of the last century this was a very popular area of study in both testaments, though less so now. From an Old Testament perspective, this study looks at what is definitely predicted and promised in the Old Testament in terms of the end of an age and the ushering in of a new age. A third possibility is to take a more literary approach and look at the medium of apocalyptic writing as a literary genre, to see what prompted it and how it can best be interpreted today. Vi would probably be most interested in that.

As we have already noted, the predominant critical method used with regard to the prophets is a historical one that relates each to his historical environment. It is not difficult, using that method, to make a case for 'forth-telling' in a contemporary context. Although we have to be careful not to accept the view of society provided by the eighth-century BC prophecies of Amos or Micah as the only view possible, when we come to the longer books of the Latter Prophets we have more overt opportunity to relate them to political events. The book of Isaiah contains several specific historical references (e.g. the death of King Uzziah in 736 BC is noted in 6.1; the Assyrian Sennacherib's siege of Jerusalem in 701 occupies chapters 36—37; the Babylonian destruction of Jerusalem in 586 is noted in 49.19; the intervention of Cyrus of the Medes who reigned 550–530 is noted in 45.1ff.; and the rebuilding of the Temple, probably in 515, is noted in 66.1f.). A more comprehensive account is provided in Sawyer (1993, pp. 83f.).

TO DO

Read Isaiah 7.1–17. This is set during the reign of King Ahaz, when he fears the invasion of Jerusalem, and its defeat, by an alliance between Samaria and Damascus. Then read chapters 36—39, which deal with the actual siege of Jerusalem by the Assyrian Sennacherib, during the time of Hezekiah. What marked similarities and differences do you see between the accounts?

Some wish to claim that the two should be read together (Prévost, 1993, pp. 66f.; Brueggemann, 2003, p. 163) and that there is an intended contrast between Ahaz, 'a model of unfaith' (Brueggemann, 2003, p. 161), and Hezekiah, who 'did what was right in the eyes of the LORD, as his ancestor David had done' (2 Kings 18.3). What do you think? What bearing does your answer have on the following issue?

Isaiah 7 contains one of the most famous predictive passages in the Old Testament. Verse 14 predicts: 'A young woman is with child, and she will give birth to a son and call him Immanuel.' Consideration of this passage reveals the difficulties of distinguishing between prediction, and commentary more immediately relevant to the prophet's own time. The Gospel of Matthew takes the passage as predictive of the birth of Jesus (Matthew 1.22f.), which acts as a fulfilment of this prophecy and, standing as it does at the beginning of the New Testament, as a model to the reader of how Old Testament prophecy is to be understood by Christians. In fact the verse does not bear all the weight Matthew wishes to place on it. The Hebrew word *almah*, used in Isaiah 7.14, means something like the old English word *damsel*, and does not imply virginity in a technical sense. In the Greek translation of the Hebrew Scriptures current at the time of Matthew, known as the Septuagint, the Greek word used to translate *almah* is *parthenos*, which does imply virginity. Thus, in so far as Matthew's argument is about virginity, it fails; but what about the wider significance of a child who will symbolize God's presence?

The point here is that there is a very evident explanation of who the Immanuel of Isaiah is, from within the text itself. First, it is notable that in the Hebrew text the word *almah* is preceded by the definite article, denoting both particularity and respect. So who could this be? The two main possibilities are the prophet's wife or the wife of the king. The following chapters, 7—11, which remind readers of the promise of 7.14, namely 9.6f. and chapter 11 (initially vv. 1–10), describe the child in royal terms and ascribe a political task to him. The announcement itself is comparable to the announcements of other remarkable births of important people (Genesis 16.11; 18.10;

Judges 13.5). Also every time the prophet uses the word 'sign' he does so with local reference (Prévost, 1993, p. 65). This all adds up, in the view of many, to identifying the child of 7.14 with Hezekiah, son of Ahaz, and possibly comparable with him, as in the Isaiah 'To do' exercise above.

So we could argue that the prophecies of eighth-century Isaiah can all be ascribed to current political circumstances. The prophecies of exile Isaiah relate to the returning exiles, and the prophecies of post-exile Isaiah relate to the building of the Temple by the returning Judah-ites or Jews. But that is not sufficient. A number of passages in exile Isaiah, usually known as Servant Songs or Songs of the Suffering Servant, do not admit of easy identification with contemporary people and events. Indeed, they appear to have a more universal and profound point to make (Isaiah 42.1–9; 49.1–6; 50.4–9; 52.13—53.12). It is easy to see why these passages were used by early Christian apologists, whose task it was to persuade a doubting religious constituency that 'it was written' that the Messiah should suffer (Lindars, 1961, pp. 77ff.). However, Brueggemann, summarizing recent scholarship reports, 'that the "servant" in these four poems, like the "servant" elsewhere in the poetry of Second Isaiah, is none other than Israel' (Brueggemann, 2003, p. 169). In other words, the *intention* of the author was not to foretell the manner of the ministry and death of Jesus but to describe the post-exilic vocation of Israel. Literary critics would argue that that does not exhaust the matter, and that different generations can legitimately find truth in the texts beyond the intention of the original author; and that indeed the concept of inspiration has meaning in that way. However, by definition that is beyond academic proof. What we can claim to know is the original intention, whatever we make of it.

An important part of any serious study of the Old Testament is to think about what we mean by inspiration. What does it mean to say that these texts are the inspired word of God? Our answer to that question will have a bearing on how we read the text, but more importantly, how we respond to the way critics read the text. If we take the extreme view that effectively God dictated the word into the minds of writers, then the text has an importance for us that it did not have, for example, for later Jewish scholars. Also, if the truth contained in texts is dependent, for us, on the answer to the question concerning what really happened, then any suggestion that what is described did not 'happen' is likely to be rejected as contravening our idea of inspiration.

TO DO

Think about what inspiration means for you. And what difference does this make to the point at which you would become defensive? In previous chapters we have seen challenges to the historical accuracy of, for example: the creation of the world in seven days; the existence of two people called Adam and Eve in the Garden of Eden; the conquest of Jericho; the settlement of Israel in a single triumphant move and the ethnic make-up of 'Israel'. Which of these do you find the most challenging and what tensions do you feel as a scholar as a result?

Think about how you would use the term 'inspired' in other contexts and to describe secular literature. In literary studies, inspiration is what is reckoned to give work a reference to generations way beyond the original writer's, and also beyond his or her intentions. Is that helpful in thinking about biblical inspiration?

In the same way we can describe with some confidence the original intention of Isaiah as providing, in its final edition, a three-part journey from the prospect of exile to the rebuilding of Jerusalem, with the new theological insights already noted about the lessons to be learned from the experience of exile. In particular it demonstrates one theological strand of response, namely the sense of hopefulness that Jerusalem itself will become a positive religious symbol and tradition. We can see the original intention of Jeremiah and other prophets of the seventh century as providing warnings, reflections and assurances connected with the impending crisis, which eventually struck in 597 and 587. The exilic and post-exilic prophets are concerned with rebuilding and with learning appropriate lessons about God from the exile experience. Most of their prophecies find resolution in their own day and do not look forward to a much later time that might coincide with the end of the world. So far, Vi would be disappointed.

The prophet Ezekiel might give her new hope – Ezekiel can be very precisely dated. The book itself contains 14 precise dates for oracles, which enable us to place him exactly as a prophet of the Exile. He is a priest (1.3) and represents a response to the events of exile recognizably similar to the P tradition, calling for a new holiness (Ezekiel 28.25f.). His account of the relationship between God and Israel paints Israel as filthy rather than unjust. In chapters 16, 20 and 23 (already quoted), Israel is described as a whore. She needs to cleanse herself. Chapter 8 describes the violation of God's holiness in the Temple and so God's absence from there. The first half of the book, in fact, is taken up with condemnation, following the account of the prophet's call in chapters 1—3. Chapters 25—48 are a counterpoint, with visions of a future that feed hope. Chapters 25—32 are oracles against the nations. Chapters 33—37 contain some memorable images of promise (e.g. the picture of God's breath working among the valley of dry bones in chapter 37). Chapters 38 and 39 belong more closely to the apocalyptic tradition (see below). Chapters 40—48 describe the restored Temple. It is notable that the author of the New Testament book of Revelation draws repeatedly on the imagery of this book, and the new temple image in particular.

The most extensive recent thematic study of eschatology in the Old Testament draws particularly on the book of Ezekiel (Gowan, 2000). Gowan believes that the eschatological interest in the Prophets stems from their understanding of what is wrong with the world in the present, and evidenced through their promises of future improvement. These include washing away 'the filth' of Zion (Isaiah 4.4), an end to warfare (Micah 4.3), an end to infirmity and disease (Isaiah 35.5f.), no more hunger (Ezekiel 36.30) and the end of natural dangers such as dangerous wild animals (Isaiah 11.9). All this is summed up as an end to wickedness and sin (Jeremiah

33.8). Gowan sees no agreement among scholars on a definition of Old Testament eschatology and so suggests his own. 'I believe we shall find it helpful to consider the major theme of all the prophetic promises to be "the end of evil"' (Gowan, 2000, p. xi).

Gowan (2000) describes Ezekiel 36.22–38 as providing a model for the threefold transformation to which he believes the prophets point. There is a need to transform the human person (Ezekiel 36.25–27 – the phrase 'a heart of flesh' is particularly emblematic). There is also a need to transform human society (Ezekiel 36.24, 28, 33–36). This passage makes reference to Jerusalem and highlights its importance as a cultic centre. This is a typical P approach. However, it does find common cause with the D theology that sees Jerusalem as a centre of excellence and the dwelling place of good kings, and with the Isaiah Zion tradition, which finds echoes in the Psalms (e.g. Psalms 46; 122). The final kind of transformation that is required is the transformation of nature itself (Ezekiel 36.30, 35).

TO DO

Read the following passages from the Psalms (2.6; 46.2; 68.18; 74.13–17; 76.1–12; 78.68; 87.1; 93.3f.; 96.6–9; 132.13–18; 147.12–20) and make a list of the attributes of Zion that are described there. Does this help to make more sense of a hope for a new Jerusalem? Think of any hymns or songs that mention Jerusalem. How faithful are they, do you think, to the dreams of the Psalmists?

The transformation of the *human person* needs to come about through a new awareness of forgiveness, creating a new person. The transformation of *society* means restoration to a promised land, which is also described in terms of defeat of the nations followed by peace with the nations and the rule of a righteous king. The transformation of *nature* means abundant fertility, a new natural order and effectively a new earth. We might note that these ideals and promises are intimately bound up with the experience of exile and the possibility that return gives to the people to make a fresh start. Two broad theological options were effectively open to the exiles. One was to concentrate on what we might call a 'theology of return'. The other was to work out a 'theology of sojourn'. They opted for the former. But that is not to say that they had not learned theological lessons from the experience of foreign sojourn. As already noted, the most important concerned monotheism.

We have seen the results of this new theological 'discovery' in terms of creation theology and how it led to the writings we think of as the Wisdom literature. We have noted the creative energy evidenced in the book of Proverbs, unleashed by the idea that wisdom was part of God's creative plan, and so human behaviour and responses can teach us something about God's purposes. There is a darker side to the Wisdom literature though, evidenced by the book of Job, which wants to know why creation allows good people to suffer. Surely in a perfectly created world that would not be the case. Alongside the thinking about the creation of the natural world was awareness that a creator God must also be responsible for ordering and planning human society and history. History must also have been designed. Moreover, that direction of thought can combine with the concerns that found expression in the book of Job to create an answer to the problem of suffering along the lines of suffering being a symptom of this present age: an age that is passing away. God has designed history to operate in a series of stages and so this suffering is a part of God's plan and design, the purpose of which is to point to the end of this age and the imminent dawn of a new one (Holdsworth, 2005, pp. 142f.). That is a way of treating history that also responds to the Prophets' concern about how a 'designed history' could contain so much violence, corruption and injustice. This strand of theological thinking finds expression especially in the literary genre of apocalyptic.

Apocalyptic is a form of popular literature that derives from a Jewish culture in the two centuries before Christ and the first century AD. The term 'apocalyptic' means revelation. What is said to be revealed in these writings are the ultimate truths about life. The presumed author is given a privileged view of God's plan for history, which the author in turn reveals to the readers. This plan is set out according to common rules of apocalyptic writing and contains a theology that is also common to them. The vast majority of apocalypses are Jewish but this form was also used by Christian writers and identifiable elements of it are to be found in the New Testament (e.g. Mark 13; Matthew 24; Luke 17; Revelation). Apocalyptic is not easy for us to read. It has a 'science fiction' feel about it. In so far as it claims to deal in holy secrets it is open to a wide variety of misreadings from those who want religion to be mysterious and to contain messages only accessible to the initiated.

TO DO

What does the term 'apocalyptic' mean to you? Can you think of instances where you have heard it used recently? Look through a newspaper to see if you can see it there. It is generally used to describe utter devastation in terms of warfare, natural disaster, famine and disease. At the end of this session, think about whether, and how, you feel the term is being misused in today's culture.

Indeed, one of the features of apocalyptic is that it claims that kind of esotericism. It claims to be making secret things known. The works are pseudonymous – that is, we do not know who wrote them – but they usually claim to have been written by someone with stature in the tradition. People with some kind of mystery attaching to them were particularly popular. So, for example, Enoch, one of two people in the Old Testament who did not die (the other is Elijah). According to Genesis 5.22, 'Enoch walked with God, and then was seen no more, because God had taken him away.' Enoch is an obvious pseudonymous title. Others include Adam, Noah, Isaiah and Moses. These are people who were believed to have a history of special insight into God's purposes.

The puzzling aspects of apocalyptic derive from the use of symbolism – some of which is taken from the mythology of other cultures – and from the conventions of writing that take us on journeys through heaven or the realm of the dead. These findings emphasize the connections between earth and heaven by switching between them as scenes in which God's drama is acted out, and in which angels are able to move from earth to heaven and vice versa almost at will. In the Old Testament the only developed apocalypse is contained in the book of Daniel, written around 163 BC. There are apocalyptic passages in some other books, including Isaiah 24—27, Ezekiel 38—39 and Zechariah 7—14. Despite not being greatly evidenced, apocalyptic writing is nonetheless important as it draws together several strands of post-exilic thinking and provides a number of concepts that are used as tools by New Testament writers to describe the significance of Jesus. These include Kingdom of God, Parousia, Resurrection, Messiah, Son of Man and Day of Judgement.

Among the internal features of apocalyptic writing we can mention the following. They are determinist, based on the idea that God has a plan that will not be shifted off course. God is accepted to be a distant character, making God more mysterious. God has a range of intermediaries or angels, some of which have specific portfolios, rather like a parliamentary cabinet. Health is Raphael, Communication is Gabriel and Defence/Warfare is Michael, for example. These writings often display a dualistic view of creation not seen elsewhere in the Old Testament. Good and evil really are fighting a war here, and God needs God's troops to keep faith and stay pure. There is a very strong moral tone, not unlike that in modern science fiction. Salvation is seen much more in terms of rescuing good people from trouble than rescuing fallen people from sin.

For the first time we see the development of a life after death. Hitherto when people died they went to a shadowy place of non-life somewhere in the earth, called Sheol (Psalms 18.4f.; 55.15; 139.8). The Hebrew word for death, *Mot*, is the name of a Canaanite god, and there may be some cultural transference in texts where death appears personified, as at Psalm 49.14. Death has to be seen in the light of the Old Testament view of life, which is that God's breath gives life and it is God's gift to impart or withdraw (Ezekiel 37.5; cf. Job 1.21). The prospect of life after death has to be seen in the overall picture of making sense of suffering. If the apocalyptic solution is to reverse the fortunes of sufferers in the next age, then the question arises: 'What about those sufferers who died unjustly?' Life after death thus becomes a time of moral reckoning, and associated with the Day of the Lord tradition, which we saw in Amos (5.18ff.). There are just three references in the Old Testament to life after death in this more modern sense; all from the apocalyptic writings. They are Isaiah 25.6–9, 26.19 and Daniel 12.2. None of these speak of a resurrection of good people to heaven. They speak rather of a new Jerusalem and of resurrection in a general sense. Heaven remains exclusively the domain of God.

TO DO

Walter Brueggemann writes: 'The Old Testament is for the most part quite reluctant to speculate about life beyond death. When it does speak about such matters, however, the subject is YHWH's reliability, power and fidelity in the face of every threat' (Brueggemann, 2002, p. 49). Does this conclusion surprise you? Is it at odds with what you yourself believe about life after death?

The connected ideas of a Kingdom of God and a Messiah, similarly, refer to something worldly rather than otherworldly. They are the institutions of the new age, when justice will finally be restored and life will be free and fair, as God intended it in the creation of the present age, which is passing away. Various passages (e.g. Isaiah 9.2–7; 11.1–5; Jeremiah 33.14–26; Micah 5.1–6; Ezekiel 34.23; Jeremiah 30.9, 21) suggest that the idea of a new anointed one grew from a development in the idea of kingship. This Messiah is God's gift and is responsible for justice and is human. 'Messiah' is not an eschatological term in the Old Testament, or indeed a common one. However, once the Davidic line died out, after the Exile, the hope became more indeterminate and was ripe for the reinterpretation to which the intertestamental literature bears witness (see, for example, Psalms of Solomon, written around 50 BC, especially Psalm 17 and vv. 21ff.).

The emphasis on the vindication of the righteous is testimony to the contexts in which apocalyptic thrived. This was the literature of the Maccabean revolt (2 Maccabees 8) against the occupying Greeks who had defiled the Temple (2 Maccabees 4.7ff.), and in other contexts expresses the hopes of people who feel an oppressed minority. Much of the secrecy stems from the need to maintain a discipline in situations where careless talk may cost lives. The world can be easily divided into friends and enemies, and indeed most issues can be decided in black and white definite terms. Enemies are demonized and propaganda is rife. At the theological level, we hear the cry, 'How long?' (Psalm 74.10, 22f.): how long will God remain inactive and silent in the face of this threat to his people? The apocalyptic response is to say: keep calm and keep faith. God's plan is working itself out. God is in control and all will be well in the end. A righteous remnant will be rescued and the enemies of God – your enemies – will get their just reward.

TO DO

Reflect together on why you think there was a resurgence of interest in Apocalyptic writing both during and after the Second World War, and in the writings of the anti-Apartheid campaigner Alan Boesak, living in South Africa during the apartheid regime (see, for example, Boesak, 1987).

The book of Daniel derives from this Maccabean period. In Christian Bibles the book appears among the prophets but in the Hebrew Scriptures it is one of the Writings. It contains some of the familiar traits of the apocalyptic genre. These include pseudonymity (the name means 'God's judgement'), symbolic visions and esotericism. In Matthew 24.15f. we see how this esotericism is readily accepted by people in New Testament times, in a reference to Daniel 9.27. Daniel does not provide evidence of dualism; has no speculation about Heaven and

Hell; has no otherworldly journeys and no descriptions of an ideal kingdom. It does have an overall theme of maintaining hope in difficult times, in a context of pessimism born of realism.

There is evidence that Daniel is an attempt to get the reader to see the story behind the story. The word 'interpretation' is used 19 times in chapters 2, 4 and 5; and whatever the provenance of the original visions, there is a sense that they are being thought through and presented to the reader in a more accessible form (Gowan, 2001, p. 31). Daniel 9.2 presents Daniel as someone who reflects on the meaning of particular former prophecies (in this case Jeremiah 25.12). In fact chapter 9 is interesting in a number of ways. Daniel is portrayed as making a long intercessory prayer on behalf of the people (vv. 4–19), which is a summary of the faith and hope of the post-exile people. The following verses then portray Daniel almost as a model of messianic hopes, without using that terminology. But it is chapter 7 that has been most influential in New Testament times and beyond. Gowan describes this as the hinge chapter of the whole book, as it moves from accessible narrative, telling the story of a brave and faithful young man in a hostile environment, towards the more thoroughly apocalyptic visions (Gowan, 2001, p. 102).

The scheme is to divide history into four epochs, the last of which leads to the triumph of God over the forces of evil represented by 'the nations'. Note also the reference to 'a time, and times, and half a time' (v. 25), which also needs interpretation. Among the symbols used in the chapter are the following: the great sea (v. 3), beasts (vv. 3–7), horns (v. 8) and the colour white (v. 9).

TO DO

Read Daniel 7. Look again then at verses 9 and 10 and see how many different images are conjured up in just those two verses. What do you think is the effect of that build-up of images on the reader? Can you think of other places in the Old Testament where God is described using these symbols (see Exodus 19; Ezekiel 1 for ideas; also 1 Kings 22.19–22; Job 1; Isaiah 6)?

Of particular interest is Daniel 7.13, which is quoted in the New Testament by the Synoptic Gospel writers (following Mark 14.62) and by Stephen at his martyrdom (Acts 7.56). This is also the first occurrence of what was to become a tradition concerning the Son of Man. In this vision, two things are clear: first, the identification of the last little horn with the hated Antiochus IV Epiphanes; second, the promise of the vindication of the 'holy ones (of the Most High)' (vv. 18, 21f., 27) by the 'Ancient in Years' (or days), who is clearly God. In later tradition, and particularly apocalyptic tradition, the Son of Man is clearly identified as the agent of vindication for communities who feel that they have kept faith without seeing a positive outcome. It is not clear whether Daniel sees the Son of Man as a title or a similar description to the others he uses in verses 4 ('like a lion') and 5 ('like a bear'). In this case verse 13 ('one like a human being') would simply mean a human, or 'someone' (see Gowan, 2001, p. 107).

The identity of the Son of Man has been of particular interest to New Testament scholars, aware that this is the only term of self-designation to be found on Jesus' lips. The issue for them is whether this is an authentic self-understanding of Jesus or an interpretative description, reflecting the understanding of the early Church (see Burkett, 1999, for a full evaluation and bibliography). For the Old Testament or intertestamental scholar the issues are slightly different, though related. They are: was there a pre-Christian concept of Son of Man that was part of contemporary expectation, and in which direction is the 'coming' described in verse 13? Is it a bringing of the holy ones to heaven or is it a coming from heaven to earth? This too has a bearing on New Testament theological development, in that this passage appears to have been the prompt for the theology of *parousia* (a Greek word meaning coming, or being at hand, the verb from which, *pareimi*, is used in the Greek version – the Septuagint – of Daniel 7.13), and later translated by Christians to mean a second coming of Christ (see Robinson, 1957, for a thorough analysis of the concept, which has not dated). However, even in the New Testament the *parousia* concept is not linked to the few occurrences of an idea of the end of all things (e.g. 1 Peter 4.7). So the conclusion might be that Vi is disappointed.

TO DO

Is this a disappointing or an encouraging response for you? How does it correspond to the faith you brought with you to the quest? What would you like to read next, or find out more about as a result?

In fact the Bible does not speak of the end of the world in a physical sense at all. It is not essentially pessimistic, as if God has given up on the whole project, but optimistic, continually looking for new evidence of God's concern and initiative, and having a clear and hopeful imaginative view of what life in a jurisdiction that has recaptured the concept of having God as its king might be like.

Further reading

Gowan, D. E., 1976, *Bridge Between the Testaments*, Pittsburgh, PA: Pickwick Press.

Gowan, D. E., 2001, *Daniel* (Abingdon Old Testament Commentaries), Nashville, TN: Abingdon Press.

McGrath, A. E., 2003, *A Brief History of Heaven*, Oxford: Blackwell.

Prévost, J.-P., 1993, *How to Read the Apocalypse*, London: SCM Press.

Russell, D. S., 1964, *The Method and Message of Jewish Apocalyptic*, London: SCM Press.

Smith-Christopher, D., 2002, *A Biblical Theology of Exile*, Minneapolis, MN: Fortress Press.

5

Could the Old Testament be of any help to someone who is suffering?

Peggy's real name is Margaret, but everyone calls her Peggy and she is one of the best-known people in the locality as the District Nurse. She is also a member of her local church congregation, and has been since her youth. She believes she owes something of being drawn towards her present career to the stories she heard in formative years about a loving caring God and a gentle healing Jesus. When she heard the story of the Good Samaritan it just seemed to her so absolutely right that people should behave in that way. But try as she might, she has failed, until recently, to find any resource in the Old Testament that would help her in her work. She finds there only stories of an angry God, warfare and destruction. Recently, though, she has joined a Lent group looking at the book of Job, and that has prompted her curiosity to see what other resources could be there; to wonder if she has misjudged it or missed something and to ask: 'Could the Old Testament be of any help to someone who is suffering?'

TO DO

Would you have any immediate answer to Peggy's question? Is there any part of the Old Testament that you have read that has brought comfort at a difficult time? As confidentiality allows, share your answers with the group.

We shall turn to the book of Job presently, and indeed a central theme of that book is undeserved suffering and how God is to be understood or discovered in relation to situations of unjust suffering. Any treatment of suffering in the Old Testament would certainly need to take account both of Job and of portions of the book of Psalms (see the next chapter). The traditional context for those discussions is the belief that disobedience to YHWH is the cause of suffering, while obedience to YHWH brings life and delight (Deuteronomy 30.15–20; Proverbs 8.35f.). As Brueggemann points out, although this appears a simplistic view of life, it does at least include two key assertions of faith. One is that the world is morally coherent and the other is that human behaviour is morally significant (Brueggemann, 2002, p. 201). However, that is a view whose simplicity is fundamentally challenged by Job, and elsewhere, as a direct result of the growth of creation theology, in turn a result of the dreadful trauma of the Exile.

As we have seen, one of the major shifts in Old Testament study in recent years has been the new interest in the effect that the Exile had on the faith of the people (for a full discussion, see Holdsworth, 2005, pp. 36–9). That interest has been fuelled by the interest in literary approaches to criticism, by sociological insights, by new historical interest in the context of first 'publication' and by suspicion about the historical veracity of Exodus accounts. This new interest in exile has led to claims that 'exile evoked the most brilliant literature and the most daring theological articulation in the Old Testament ... grounded in a sense of and sureness of *news* about God that circumstances cannot undermine or negate' (Brueggemann, 1997, p. 3).

What Brueggemann is pointing to is the crisis for faith that the Exile represented. A people who believed their relationship with God was based on God's promise of a land, of progeny and a special relationship had seen the people driven from the land and taken to a foreign land, with every prospect of the diminution or even the extinction of their race and its particular culture. What kind of special relationship could survive that? Indeed, as many examples in the book of Jeremiah bear witness, people were giving up on the religion of YHWH because it simply did not deliver (e.g. Jeremiah

7.8–11, 18; 11.9–14; 44.15–19). The other option was to reflect on the possibility that there were new things to learn about God and new things God wanted to reveal. That is the option taken by those who wanted to continue in faith despite their experience, and it is their record that we have as the Old Testament. That is the 'daring theological articulation'.

TO DO

We have already come across the practice of eisegesis; that is, reading into a text from our own experience, which literary critics employ. Think for a moment about any experience of trauma or suffering you have experienced and then of the kind of words that might describe your feelings. Words like 'denial', 'shock', 'anger', 'helplessness' might give you a start. Keep your list, and at the end of the chapter see whether you have found examples of those feelings in the texts you read.

We cannot overestimate the extent of the trauma that the Exile represented in simple practical (brutal) terms. The narrative unfolds in 2 Kings 24.8—25.21. If we were to think of modern equivalents, affecting huge populations, we might think perhaps of the AIDS epidemic, the Holocaust, the African slave trade or the destruction of the twin towers in New York on September 11 2001. Of course these are not the kinds of suffering that Peggy has in mind, but the same kinds of feeling identified in the list above could be said to be equally evident in personal circumstances of suffering. Exile does have some particular characteristics, however. *Letters of Transit* (Aciman, 1997) describes some of them. The book is subtitled *Reflections on Exile, Identity, Language, and Loss*, and it witnesses to the need of exiled people to have their story heard and taken seriously. Both internally and externally, then, we can see the need for an account of the history of Israel. Internally as part of the search for an answer to the question, 'How could God let this happen?' Externally as a means of declaring that there *is* a history, there *is* a story and that the exiles *are* a people. The histories from both the D and P writers could be seen in this context.

Walter Brueggemann has gone further. In *Cadences of Home: Preaching Among Exiles* (1997), Brueggemann sees six responses to the experience of the Exile and then, in an eisegetical way, identifies Old Testament resources that, as he believes, are designed to meet those circumstances of exile, as he calls them, and to deal with them in a way that maintains or grows faith.

One of the circumstances of exile that he recognizes is *denial*. People operate as if all can be made right, with false hopefulness. He makes the comparison between the situation of the exiles and bereavement in all its forms. The desire that things should be different and that the hoped-for dreams can still be realized, even when it is clear that they cannot, will be recognized by those who have ministered to the bereaved or to the dying. Certainly this is the kind of situation Peggy is concerned about. The biblical resource Brueggemann identifies that responds to this is the book of Lamentations. This is a short book, full of unmitigated pain, describing in a very formal way the grief the exiles feel after the loss of Jerusalem. A recent study of Lamentations sees the same kind of denial in contemporary US society (O'Connor, 2003). Kathleen O'Connor does not find Lamentations a depressing book. Perversely, she sees it as a book that reveals pain rather than causes it, and as such is actually therapeutic: 'paradoxically, by focusing on suffering, by bringing it into the open, and reflecting it back to readers, Lamentations offers solace' (p. 4). Bereavement counsellors will know the importance of allowing people to voice their grief, even aggressively, and probably be aware of the desire, on the part of the hearer, somehow to neutralize that. That is what Lamentations does not allow. The voice of God is urgently sought but God is essentially silent.

Brueggemann and O'Connor both relate this text to modern US society, and both are concerned about denial. 'Denial refers to the refusal, perhaps even the psychic and spiritual inability, to see the horrible, to name it, to allow it space in the world' (O'Connor, 2003, p. 86). O'Connor believes that denial is at the heart of the story of original sin in Genesis 3. For her, denial is thus understood as institutionalized: 'Whether practiced by societies or individuals, denial constricts hope, depletes life, and aborts praise. Crushed spirits cannot worship unless that worship speaks from the pain' (p. 87). Brueggemann sees it as a part of the Church's vocation to be a place of honest sadness: an antidote to denial; a place that refuses to live with lies and lives in the truth. Lamentations' description of God-forsakenness is thus a pastoral model.

TO DO

Do you see any evidence of denial in today's society, or have you experienced it in a more personal or professional setting? Do you recognize O'Connor's description of its effects? Now read Lamentations 1.1–12 (and the whole chapter if you wish). Would there be anything here to help Peggy with her concerns?

Brueggemann's second 'circumstance of exile' is the sense of *being orphaned* (1997, p. 5). He points to the Old Testament genealogies, which he accepts we normally skip over as boring (see, for example, Numbers 3; 26), as a response to this; but 'The texts serve to overcome the isolation of the orphan and our sense of "motherless" existence, by giving us the names of mothers and fathers and by situating us in a "communion of saints"' (p. 6). A third circumstance is *self-preoccupation*, and here the response he sees is those books that tell a story that presents a bigger picture perspective to encourage energy and freedom, such as Daniel or Esther. Those who have spent any time with the mentally ill or depressed will recognize this element of suffering and the need to locate sufferers within a wider context. He points to Job as an antidote to what he calls *moral incongruity*, which is his way of pointing to the questions about why a good God let the calamity of the Exile happen. And 2 Isaiah is his antidote to the *power of despair*.

Whether these responses are intentional by the authors or conjectural on Brueggemann's part is certainly a question to be asked, but the kind of exercise he is engaged in does help Peggy to identify

Old Testament resources in her context. Perhaps we are on firmer ground, in the relation between intention and interpretation, when we consider his final 'circumstance' (though not the final one in his order); that is, exile produces an *experience of the absence of God*. The question is not just 'How or why could God let this happen?' It is also 'Where was God in all this?' Brueggemann notes that this sense of loss in the Old Testament context is focused on symbols of God's presence, such as the Jerusalem Temple. With its destruction, God has nowhere to dwell. The issue could then be restated: 'Where or how are we to find the presence of God when the traditional pathways have been destroyed?'

It is the P theologians that Brueggemann believes cope with this most effectively (p. 8). He points to three distinctive interests of the P writers: circumcision (Genesis 17), Sabbath observance and the traditions around the tabernacle (Exodus 25—31; 35—40). This last he describes as: 'an imaginative effort to form a special place where God's holiness can be properly hosted and therefore counted upon' (p. 8).

TO DO

Look again at the six symptoms of suffering that Brüegge-mann identifies in relation to the experience of the Exile. Do you recognize them in the experiences of suffering you have encountered – your own or someone else's – and do you feel the responses he identifies are, or could be, helpful? Are there any you would like to add? How do you respond to this way of reading the Old Testament and using its texts?

Brueggemann's three emphases in fact all become marks of national or ethnic distinctiveness, and that is important to a people who have recently had to think about what it means to be a distinctive people when they do not have a land. But these practical examples are put to use in a broader theological scheme, which sees interconnectedness and holiness as key concepts. Just as the book of Deuteronomy is said to be the manifesto for what follows in the D history, so Genesis 1, P's introduction to the Torah, is the overture to a theology that finds expression in the prophecies of Isaiah and Ezekiel, a substantial portion of the Sinai account and widely distributed throughout the Torah, but especially in the books of Leviticus and Numbers. Genesis 1 displays order and distinctiveness – each day has its own theme – but it also displays harmony. This is a creation built on delicate balances, into which humankind is introduced late and has to find its own place in a humble way.

The book of Leviticus is the ritual equivalent of that creation account. Its theology is what we would now call sacramental as it invites community members not just to listen to a word but rather to be participants in a drama or series of dramas. Worship becomes particularly important, not just in terms of thankfulness and acknowledgement of God's gifts, as in the D tradition, but in terms of realizing the holiness of God and becoming worthy of being part of creation in a society that had suffered because it had defiled the land God gave it, had not trusted God sufficiently and had opted for violence rather than harmony (Lohfink, 1994, pp. 106–14). Traditionally, 'P' has stood for 'Priestly' pointing to the supposed authors or collectors of this tradition, but to equate the contents or interest of the P tradition exclusively with priests is to do it a disservice. The holiness code in Leviticus (17—26) is directed towards lay people, and its aim is to arrive at a situation where people are all consecrated and fit to enter a consecrated land. Through ritual and worship new ways are being found of describing, in an externally observable kind of way, the distinctiveness of the people, but in a more internal way is helping those people to actualize the presence of God in a much more versatile fashion, not bounded by geography or architecture.

But it is the book of Job that Peggy expects to be most help. It presents itself as not so much a reflection on the presence of God but rather on God's nature. To set the question in classic terms (for which the technical term is 'theodicy'): if God is all good and all powerful, how can God allow good people to suffer? However, in the course of the book of Job, the distinction between the nature of God and God's presence is actually blurred. One might conclude that the most important aspect of God's nature is not so much power as desire to be alongside sufferers, in a way that we might describe as incarnational. The fact that we can use words such as 'incarnational' and 'sacramental' points to the possibility of modern application and takes us to the heart of Peggy's question, which derives from seeing the actual suffering of actual people who, in her view, have done nothing to deserve it and are often devout examples of good living.

Job is effectively a novel. It makes no pretence at a relation to historic events or context. Its opening lines might well be rendered, 'long ago in a land far away ...', and the story continues, initially in a way that flits between Job's earthly situation and the Heavenly Cabinet Room, whose members include a Minister without Portfolio called the Satan or Rover. In the first scene Job is described as a man who does everything right and who lives as near a perfectly good life as is humanly possible, according to the kind of priorities set out in the book of Proverbs. The Satan character raises a question both with God and by implication with the reader: 'Why does Job live like this?' 'What's in it for him?' Satan's nature is to think the worst of people, and he engages in a wager with God to test whether Job serves God disinterestedly or whether he only does so because 'Whatever he does you bless' (Job 1.10). God gives Satan permission to test Job.

The next scene is almost comic in its sudden series of calamities that befall Job and his family. Any 'advantages' that may have accrued from his living a blameless life are completely wiped out, so how will Job react and will Satan be proved right? The answer is 'No'. Job is not diverted: 'The LORD gives and the LORD takes away; blessed be the name of the LORD' (1.21). Satan is not satisfied. The next scene takes us back to heaven, where Satan says that his expose of Job only failed because God had imposed a condition not to harm Job himself. If this condition were lifted there would be a different result. God lifts the condition. Satan does his worst. Job becomes ill with running sores from which he can get little relief. The words that the reader wants to see are then placed in the mouth of Job's wife: 'Why do you still hold fast to your integrity? Curse God, and die!' (2.9).

Job's response is unchanged: 'If we accept good from God, shall we not accept evil?' (2.10). This response demonstrates Job's belief in what we might call the old religious certainty that there is a moral system within creation and that God is its guarantor. The author's standpoint, though, appears to be that precisely that axiom needs to be challenged, or at least set in a new context.

At this point the narrative framework is effectively abandoned, though briefly recovered in the final chapter but without any further mention of Satan or the wager. The discussion is taken forward by a series of speeches from five people, Job himself being one of them. He begins the sequence in chapter 3 with a long lament about his condition. He has been joined by three other people who each make their contribution from a slightly different perspective. Each subscribes to the old religious certainties about a moral system that rewards the good and punishes the bad. One of the points the author clearly wants to make is that, however unpalatable, the wager scenario paints a picture of God; that is, the kind of picture, or something very much like it, that the old view must inevitably hold to. 'As flies to wanton boys are we to the gods. They kill us for their sport', as Shakespeare puts it (*King Lear* 1.4.36).

Initially three of them contribute. The first, and therefore probably the eldest, is Eliphaz. He relies on experience for his view that the righteous do not suffer (cf. Psalm 37.25–28). Suffering is the result of sin, and it is no use living in denial about that. He backs up his view by reference to a vision he has had. The second friend, Bildad, who is probably younger (8.2), supports the basic argument by reference to tradition. This is the faith as received. Who are we to know better (8.8–10)? The third friend is Zophar. He uses the jargon of the new creation theology to try to persuade Job (11.5–12), which is deeply ironic because it is precisely the questions raised by that theology that the book is concerned with.

TO DO

From your experience, have you ever met these or similar responses to your suffering?

- When you've been around as long as I have ...
- I have prayed about it and God has said ...
- Well, the Church believes ...
- From a theological point of view there's a much bigger picture ...
- I'm sure it's all for a purpose ...

What was your response? How do you now expect Job to respond?

In each case Job makes a dismissive response, culminating in the retort of 12.6, which though difficult to translate can be read (as, for example, RSV): 'The tents of robbers are at peace, and those who pro-voke God are secure, who bring their god in their hand.' This would be consistent with Job's general approach, that a mechanistic view of God's relation to suffering relegates God to an idol. If God is fully understood and works according to a system that is fully understood, God ceases to be God. Job's appeal is basically to his experience, and he demands that that be taken seriously (13.1–5). In the process he wants to cut out the interpretative views of his friends and speak with God direct. There is a second cycle of speeches. Job is accused of arrogance in the face of experience by Eliphaz (15.7–10). Bildad, convinced that Job must have sinned, sets out a dire picture of the consequences of denial (18.11–14). Zophar still claims the spirit of wisdom (20.3) but continues to subscribe to the 'old' view. Job continues to feel that he is not being heard and that his experience is being dismissed (21.3). A third cycle of speeches makes no further progress. Chapters 29 and 30 come closest to the kind of denial of which he is accused as he longs for the old days in a way that comes close to self-pity. A new participant, Elihu, is introduced in chapter 32. Commentators regard him as an unnecessary intrusion into the text. Chapter 38 and beyond finally see God respond to Job directly from a whirlwind.

The answer is not what either Job or the reader has been led to expect. God does not answer Job's complaints but rather wrong-foots him with a dazzling description of the created universe. The vehicle for this is a series of rhetorical questions that have the effect of giving Job insight into the vastness of the creator. In a sense this vision vindicates what Job has been saying all along – that God cannot be measured or reduced to human systems or mechanical responses. But it also has the effect of humbling Job and turning him from the self-obsession of the sufferer to the reality of the vastness of God's will. Verse 42.6 is crucial, and may include a wordplay. The Hebrew verb describing the change of mind, *n ch m*, is a combination of the letters of the word at the heart of the original wager, 'disinterestedly': *ch n m* (see van Wolde, 1997, p. 139).

The fact that Job discerns God's voice outside of religious systems and interpretations is enough for him. It may be that 'the whirlwind' is in fact the experience of his own pain. In any case, the author feels he has done his job. A short narrative conclusion ratifies Job's position. From the point of view of narrative construction, the denouement is significant in that we, the reader, have been encouraged throughout to see Job as the misfit. But it is Job's friends who are finally described (by God) as those who 'have not spoken as you ought about me' (42.7). Then they too are forgiven.

Actually we do not know who the author of the book is, or his background, though his question is thought to suggest his context. It is interesting that only in the Prologue and when God speaks is God named as YHWH. Elsewhere God is known by a variety of names, including El, Shaddai and Eloah. This may suggest that Job and his friends are non-Israelites (so Whybray, 1998, p. 157) or there may be a more sophisticated purpose in replacing 'old' and national, or even tribal, names for God with a modern international one, demonstrating what the narrative discloses: that YHWH is the God of all creation.

Those, like Brueggemann, who take the experience of the Exile as their starting point would describe the purpose of the author as being a post-exilic man of faith who has seen the implications of believing in a good creator God, while experiencing the imperfections of that creation in terms of unjust suffering, either nationally as in the Exile (and as introduced by Habakkuk 1.13) or perhaps individually. So the aim of the writer is that he wants to believe that the creation is morally coherent and that behaviour is morally significant. Others such as Eaton (1985) believe the key theme is whether disinterestedness is actually possible. Whybray (1998) believes the book is an attempt to let God be God, and to describe realistically the difficulty of discerning God's ways. Van Wolde (1997) thinks the point of the book is not so much to vindicate Job as to describe his own journey towards a new perspective: 'He no longer needs to know God's unfathomable nature. He is freed from the false expectations which are aroused by the old idea of retribution and reward and which have misled his friends' (1997, p. 3).

For modern purposes, and particularly for Peggy's purposes, the book offers some models of pastoral practice. Faced with suffering individuals who can be angry or inconsolable or even violent, the tendency is to want to speak rather than listen.

TO DO

What do you think would be the main lessons Peggy might draw from this discussion that would help her in her pastoral work?

If Job offers one innovative and, in its way, stunning contribution to the issue of suffering, then 2 Isaiah offers another. Isaiah 40—55 is the basic undisputed deposit of the material from this prophet of the Exile, though it may extend further and editors may have displaced some of his oracles into earlier sections of Isaiah. It is natural for there to be a link between suffering and creation theology, since the presence of suffering suggests a flawed creation. Two important contributions are included in 2 Isaiah. The first is to see the link between comfort from suffering and divine forgiveness. Isaiah

40 begins with the words 'Comfort my people; ... proclaim to her that her term of bondage is served, her penalty is paid, for she has received at the LORD's hand double measure for all her sins' (40.1f.).

The forgiveness mentioned here is of a different order from that which has become part of liturgical life, in which restitution and repentance followed by sacrifice and confession restore relations between neighbours (e.g. Leviticus 4.22–35). There is, in the post-exile period, a sense of the enormity of the sin of Israel among those who believe that was the cause of the Exile. There is also a greater awareness of the residual presence of evil, which is greater than transactions between persons. Texts such as Jeremiah 24.4–7, Ezekiel 36.31 and 39.25–27 bear witness to this. The Sinai tradition makes it clear that forgiveness is part of YHWH's nature (Exodus 34.6f.), but the way this has been used in the tradition in connection with ideas of natural justice means that just as those ideas of justice have to be rethought, as in Job, so does the idea of forgiveness. Gowan describes what is needed as 'eschatological forgiveness', a form of forgiveness that deals radically and cosmically with sin and evil, and sees examples in 2 Isaiah.

> In the exuberant language of 2 Isaiah, the thoroughness of that new kind of forgiveness which is celebrated is described by the verb *m ch h* (wipe away), among others (Isa. 43:25; 44:22). As far as God is concerned, then, those sins are just gone. (Gowan, 2000, p. 64).

In modern pastoral language that means that there is a real acceptance that a line has been drawn and the past is truly erased.

The second is contained in the series of four so-called servant songs already noted (Isaiah 42.1–4; 49.1–6; 50.4–9; 52.13—53.12), in which a servant of God has a vocation to suffering that actually has a redemptive effect. In other words, suffering can bring good. Suffering can be for a reason. Scholarly work on these songs has concentrated on attempts at identifying the servant, which is probably Israel, and an argument about whether this text belongs to Judaism or Christianity. Was this text always 'intended' to point towards Jesus and his atoning passion, or did the early Church find an interpretative medium for that death in these passages? However, there is here an important new understanding about suffering that should not be overlooked.

Peggy recognizes both these elements from her own experience. She knows that much suffering is caused by accrued guilt, and she knows the comfort that can come from reconciliation. She is also aware, particularly in the immediate aftermath of a tragedy, say the death of a child as the result of a medical mistake, that people, parents in this case, want the death to matter. They want something to change as a result of it. They want good to emerge from bad. They find comfort in the thought that as a result of this death, procedures will change and others will not have to suffer. It is little surprise that New Testament theologians, trying to make sense of the death of Jesus, should look to these passages and subsequently include them in their own apologetic.

TO DO

Can you think of ways in which nowadays people want a death to matter, and to make a difference? You might look through a newspaper for examples. Are you convinced that redemptive suffering is possible? What does that say to you about God?

Bearing in mind all that this chapter has described, and imagining Peggy reading it, how do you think she might answer her own question?

Further reading

Cox, H. and Paulsell, S., 2012, *Lamentations and the Song of Songs* (Belief Commentaries), Louisville, KY: Westminster John Knox Press.

Eaton, J. H., 1985, *Job* (Old Testament Guides), Sheffield: JSOT Press.

Lohfink, N., 1994, *Theology of the Pentateuch: Themes of the Priestly Narrative and Deuteronomy*, Edinburgh: T. & T. Clark.

O'Connor, K. M., 2003, *Lamentations and the Tears of the World*, Maryknoll, NY: Orbis Books.

6

Can the Old Testament worship texts make a contribution to church life and understanding today?

Peggy's best friend is Edith. They have similar views on most things and both are committed members of their local church and attend the monthly Bible study group. Edith has followed the answer to Peggy's question with interest. She heads the church's pastoral care team but is also a worship leader. As such she is aware that most services she takes part in or devises contain a Psalm from the Old Testament, usually read together by the congregation rather than by just one person. She thinks of the book of Psalms as like an ancient hymnbook that still has meaning today. Also, on some special occasions, notably Harvest Festival, she is aware of readings, from the book of Deuteronomy in particular, that describe ancient rituals and yet speak to the modern occasion. Her question seeks to combine her interest in contemporary worship with the pastoral life of the church as she seeks a joined-up way of being a church member who values and uses the Scriptures. Her question is: 'Can the Old Testament worship texts make a contribution to church life and understanding today?'

TO DO

Do you identify with Edith's description of the book of Psalms as being like an ancient hymnbook? If so, how does it differ from a modern hymnbook? The most obvious answer might be that there seems to be no principle of organization behind it. Is this a problem for you? If you were to try to 'organize' the Psalms, how might you do it? (You would in fact be following the same path as Hermann Gunkel, below.)

The book of Psalms is the first in the third canon that forms the Hebrew Scriptures, the Writings, and that probably points to its importance within Jewish religion. For hundreds of years Jewish commentators interpreted the book in terms of messianic expectation, and it was commonplace before the rise of critical scholarship for Christians to read the Psalms in a Christological way, as if spoken by Jesus himself. Academic scholarship has for the past two hundred years been more concerned with the historical setting of the Psalms and the literary conventions they exemplify. In the early part of the twentieth century, two scholars in particular determined the direction of study. Hermann Gunkel, influenced both by enthusiasm for form criticism and by a Germanic aptitude for organization, attempted a classification of the Psalms that is still a standard starting point for scholars.

Gunkel classified the Psalms with headings such as Hymns, Songs of Zion, Royal Psalms, Liturgies, Thanksgivings and Laments. Others have followed the methodology, using slightly different or nuanced headings, but the basic work remains as a major contribution to Old Testament studies. Following the conventions of form criticism, Gunkel sought to identify genres among the Psalms and then to ascribe to each a setting in real life (*Sitz im Leben*). To decide on genres he was concerned with 'opportunities for worship' and with 'the common treasure of concepts and moods' (as quoted by Gerstenberger, 2001, p. 403). One of his early conclusions was that the Psalms were primarily liturgical and communal and not individual literary constructions, and this remains the conviction of the majority of scholars. Authorship, for example, is not thought to be an issue. One writer compares them with so-called Negro Spirituals that developed in particular settings in a communal way (Brueggemann, 2003, p. 279). Unfortunately Gunkel's publishing dates of the early twentieth century coincided with great interest in the history of religions and biblical archaeology, which led study of the Psalms away from theology and towards history, with attempts to further refine the actual historical setting of each Psalm. Sigmund Mowinckel, a student of Gunkel's, continued his work, concentrating on the kind of cultic occasions that may have helped the Psalms develop, with particular emphasis on the New Year festival, involving the enthronement of the king.

In the later twentieth century there is evidence of many critical approaches to the Psalms (see Gerstenberger in Perdue (ed.), 2001, pp. 404f.). The rise of new literary critical approaches has stimulated a new interest in the forms of Hebrew poetry and their rhetorical strategies (e.g. Robert Alter, 1998, pp. 230ff.). It has also led to studies on particular genres that Gunkel identified (e.g. Westermann, 1981), as well as new attempts to superimpose other perspectives on Gunkel's framework (e.g. Brueggemann, 1984, 2014). It is possible to reduce Gunkel's categories to four main ones. They would be the Hymn, the Song of Thanksgiving, the Individual Lament and the Communal Lament. The first two, expressed in the first-person plural and singular respectively (though, like Negro Spirituals perhaps, not necessarily for individual use), speak positively of life experience and express thanksgiving and praise.

The Laments speak from the opposite pole, of life experience overwhelmed by suffering. It may seem perverse to approach the Psalms from the direction of an experience of suffering. Many of our best-known Psalms, especially those that have been given metrical transformation into hymns, appear to have praise at their heart rather than suffering (e.g. Psalm 72: 'Jesus shall reign where'er the Sun', 'Hail to the Lord's Anointed'; Psalm 103: 'Praise my Soul the King of Heaven'; Psalm 150, 'O Praise ye the Lord'; and, most famously of all, Psalm 23, 'The Lord's my Shepherd'). However, a closer examination of the 150 Psalms shows their great variety and also, perhaps, makes us more aware of just how many Psalms do in fact speak of suffering.

Laments actually form by far the largest single section of the Psalms, including around a third of the total work. Westermann (1981) has set out the basic structure of Laments. They have remarkable features, as further work by Miller (2013) and Brueggemann (2014) has suggested.

First, they are brutally honest in their description of suffering, and in the feelings of the authors about those deemed responsible. This robustness often prompts uneasiness in the modern reader who believes such unrestrained negative emotion is at odds with religious sentiment. Psalm 109, for example, describes the suffering the author has endured at the hands of 'the wicked'. He has apparently been falsely accused, by someone to whom he was close, to whom he showed love even. As a result he is 'downtrodden and poor' and his 'flesh wastes away' because he is too poor to buy food and because he has to endure the taunts of opponents. But the heart of the Psalm is a wish list of vengeful curses upon those responsible (vv. 8–20). 'There is nothing polite or deferential about lament prayer' (Brueggemann, 2014, p. 92). For Brueggemann, this demonstrates faith rather than its opposite – a faith that God is robust enough to 'take' the complaint, and a faith that believes nothing need be hid from a God who has no need to be shielded. Moreover this has the effect of clearing the air and allowing the writer to move on. As my daughter has always apparently believed: 'A problem shared is a problem dumped.'

TO DO

Read Psalm 109. For Edith this is a new experience. She is not familiar with reading this kind of thing publicly and feels quite embarrassed about it. She does see the point that Brueggemann is making though, and recognizes from her own experience the importance of honest statement of our feelings. What is your view on this? Do you think the intensity of these writings makes them more, or less, 'holy'?

Second, this is but one example of a wider tendency to present a message that is counter to modern culture as some – particularly US – writers see it, as we have already observed in our reference to Lamentations. These writers see that culture as being one of denial, despair, anxiety, self-sufficiency and without norms. The Psalms in contrast present a world in terms of trustful fidelity, abrasive truth-telling, dependence, hope and lively remembering, and with norms of fidelity (e.g. Brueggemann, 2014, pp. 10–26).

Third, it is remarkable that praise alternates with bitterness and cursing. This may be due to the supposed therapeutic possibilities of abrasive truth-telling, but in some cases the movement from one to the other, from complaint to praise, is particularly abrupt. Between verses 21 and 22 of Psalm 22, for example, there is a massive shift. The first part of the Psalm is a complaint from the depths of God-forsakenness. Then suddenly we read, 'I shall declare your fame to my associates' as the introduction to a section of praise. What Brueggemann describes as the 'dominant scholarly hypothesis' (2003, p. 282) is that in a situation of public worship, at this point in the recital of the Psalm an oracle of assurance was delivered, such as Isaiah 43.1f. or Jeremiah 30.10f., with its dominant theme of: Do not be afraid for I am with you.

Fourth, what is really remarkable is that these Psalms are juxtaposed with very different confident and 'happy' songs. Brueggemann accounts for this by suggesting a reading strategy for the Psalms that sees a journey in three parts (Brueggemann, 1984). The journey begins with the naïve child of creation theology: happy settledness. All the problems of a creation theology held by the well-to-do and powerful are exemplified by Psalms such as Psalms 33 and 37. It is the righteous who are addressed (v. 1). Those who attempt to disturb the settledness of creation will be frustrated (v. 10). All has gone well with the people addressed because they *are* righteous and have understood the rules of creation and kept them. By implication those who have not done so well or who agitate for change have only themselves to blame (Psalm 37.25).

TO DO

Read Psalms 33 and 37. With whom do you identify in these Psalms? Is it 'the righteous', those who agitate for change or those begging bread who get what they deserve?

A very different perspective is described by the majority of the Psalms, which speak from an experience of lost innocence and whose easy view of natural justice has been demolished by personal loss. Psalm 69 would be an example, as would Psalm 22, quoted in the Passion Narrative of the New Testament. These describe the experience of the real world. They articulate it before God and, as argued above, thereby demonstrate a kind of faith. The threefold journey is completed with the kind of Psalm that Brueggemann describes in terms of reorientation, which demonstrates the whole movement from a childlike belief, through the adolescence of troubledness to a new assurance in maturity; Psalm 30 would be an example. This scheme can be applied in a number of ways: in terms of religious growth and development, as above, but also in historical perspective, describing pre-exile Israel, exile experience and post-exile experience. They speak to Edith in terms of the stages of bereavement. Brueggemann himself does not press these kinds of application. But what we may be seeing here is a replica of the movement towards healing that we saw in Job: the movement from self-absorption to dependence. Lament claims self against God. Thanksgiving cedes self to God (Brueggemann, 2014, pp. 3f.).

The analysis is suggestive in other ways. If it is part of modern critical consensus that the Old Testament, as a creative enterprise, came together as a result of the experience of the Exile, then we might look with fresh eyes at the introduction to the whole volume; that is, the first 11 chapters of Genesis. We have become accustomed to stories of Adam and Eve that have lent an almost benign air to the whole episode. It is the stuff of stand-up comedy. Illustrations in children's books show shapely Eves and six-pack Adams. But if we look beneath that domestication of the texts, what we see are three quite sophisticated theological observations about how societies break down. One is that innocence is lost; another is that moral boundaries are not observed; the third is that violence is always a symptom of sin. That is what 'the Fall' amounts to in real life, and in a sense that is also what the Psalms are saying and attempting to play their part in repairing. There is something here, then, that chimes with both the created order and our experience of the social world.

TO DO

Read Psalm 88. Can you think of a community for whom that Psalm would be useful in worship? What might the use of that psalm tell us about the community's relationship with God?

Edith is quite right that there are, outside the Psalms, many Old Testament references to and prescriptions about worship. Most of this material is in the books of Exodus, Leviticus, Numbers and Deuteronomy. The reasons for worship in these books could be described under four headings. First, there is the ritual of thankfulness for deliverance from slavery and by extension for the gift of the land. Thanksgiving is due to God for redemption, liberation and the creation of successful social society. It is related to a proper sense of humility (e.g. Deuteronomy 8.17f.) and to an acceptance that the land is in fact YHWH's land held in trust in some way by the people (cf. Leviticus 25.23f.). Deuteronomy provides examples of this. The kind of readings Edith has sometimes chosen for Harvest Festival services include Deuteronomy 8.7–20; 26.1–11; and 28.1–14. A second heading is intimately related to the first, and that is covenant. Deuteronomy 8.18 makes the link explicit. The difference is that it is the Covenant itself that is the focus of the worship. Adjacent to the description of the establishment of the Covenant (Exodus 20.1—24.18) is a long section (25.1—40.38) dealing with the tabernacle and tent of meeting, together with instructions about their construction and use. There are also rituals that describe the acceptance of the Covenant and the rehearsal of its demands and promises. Some of these coincide with a festival to celebrate the accession of the king.

Then, third, there are rituals deriving from the P tradition particularly that are concerned with maintaining purity and dealing with sin, corruption and uncleanness. Leviticus 16 is a good resource for this material. Chapters 1—5 of Leviticus describe the gifts or offerings that the people must bring to the sanctuary as evidence of their commitment to holiness. That evidence includes the very detailed preparations of any specific gift (e.g. Leviticus 2.4–6), which can read like a modern cookery manual. Chapters 17—27 relate those gifts to practical covenant-inspired action. Chapter 16 is pivotal. Verses 20–22 contain the attempt to find a solution to dealing with the community's sins in terms of ritually transferring them to a goat, which will be turned out into the wilderness – the 'scapegoat'. There follows the establishment and rules for keeping the so-called Day of Atonement (more properly the Day of Purification), which is to be held in the seventh month. The seventh month is of course the Sabbath month (16.31). What the community yearns for is for God to look again at God's creation and again declare it to be good. The Sabbath connection is maintained in the idea of the Jubilee year, following seven times seven of years, in which debts are forgiven and land is returned to its original owner in recognition that it is all YHWH's anyway.

And alongside all these, fourth, are the creation-inspired ancient agrarian festivals of seedtime and harvest, probably originally designed to keep the world both safe and fertile, some of which have been overlaid with fresh meaning and reference.

Exodus 23.14–17 describes three festivals related to the agrarian year. The next mention of these festivals is at Exodus 34.18, 22. By this time the Feast of Unleavened Bread has been overlaid with observance of the Sabbath, and the Harvest Festival is called the Feast of Weeks. By the time of Deuteronomy 16, the Feast of Unleavened Bread has become the Passover, with a detailed overlay relating to the Passover account. The harvest Feast of Weeks is specifically related to the need for humility and social responsibility on the grounds of remembering that the people now settled in the land were once themselves homeless slaves (16.12). In other words, this feast now has a specific justice element. The Feast of Booths maintains this and emphasizes the characteristic Deuteronomy themes of celebration and blessing (16.14f.). Blessing is a process whereby the creation promises of material well-being, success, abundance and posterity are enacted, often by a priest. Clearly they have a specific place in liturgical life (Deuteronomy 28.3–8). The ritual for the three festivals is further developed at Leviticus 23. However, the narrative of Exodus is still central, as is the concern for the poor and needy (Leviticus 23.22). Numbers 28 and 29 add further detail.

It is likely that before the Exile the pre-eminent festival was the last, the autumn festival of Ingathering, Tabernacles or Booths. During the twentieth century there was great interest in the theological and national significance of this festival. In particular there was interest in the role of the king. The accepted position is that this was also the New Year festival in which prosperity and fertility were implored for the coming year, and that this was also then a festival in which the covenant requirements were in some way rehearsed and the king annually enthroned as a kind of guarantor of YHWH's presence and interest in YHWH's people. The so-called Enthronement Psalms (e.g. 93; 97; 99) are the main biblical evidence for this interpretation. After the Exile, with no king, the Passover feast becomes pre-eminent. This may owe something also to a growing Puritanism, which frowned on the possible excesses of a festival that also celebrated the wine harvest (see Coggins, 1990, p. 142). Judges 21 may describe something of the results of this.

Edith finds this interesting but it does not quite answer her question. She understands the kind of scholarship that can describe in historic detail what might have happened, and can understand that there are voices that regard the Bible accounts as idealized, but she has no wish to enter that debate. She also understands the theological implications of a God who redeems and who creates good things and therefore whose people need to make those activities real in their own communities. What she is less sure about is how to read passages describing ritual, such as Leviticus 1—7, in a way that could give them modern relevance or application. Does she have to leave them completely in the past, she wonders?

Samuel Balentine (2002) anticipates that problem in the Introduction to his commentary on Leviticus. He acknowledges scholarship from the direction of both history and theology but advocates an approach that perhaps owes more to anthropology. He writes: 'What is required is an imaginative construal of both the rituals described in the text – their gestural acts and symbolic words – and how their enactment has meaning within a specific understanding of the world' (Balentine, 2002, p. 3). That understanding is set out in Genesis 1, and Leviticus gives ritual structure to God's own structured creation. This is not a sterile or passive or indeed fearful response. Rather, these rituals:

> seek not only to reinforce existing assumptions about the world's order and structure. They seek also to critique status quo ways of seeing and living in the world and to alter them, in accordance with God's abiding vision, by embodying different models of behaviour that bring *what is* into conformity with God's hopes and expectations for *what should be*. (2002, p. 4; emphasis in original)

Hence they invite and become a vehicle for theological reflection on the present. Brueggemann puts it thus. 'In this approach, worship is clearly the management and enactment of symbols, in order to represent and redescribe the world in new, different, and alternative ways' (Brueggemann, 2002, p. 236).

TO DO

Can you think of any rituals or actions that happen in church that have particular meaning for you? You might think of, for example, lighting candles, passing the peace, kneeling for prayer. Are these actions more or less important for you than words?

This begins to make more sense to Edith, who belongs to a church that has its own rituals, the most central of which, Holy Communion, or the Eucharist, is enacted every week as the principal act of worship. She has heard sermons over the years in which preachers have said that this service is not just a sterile enactment but that it is a making real of something in a way that invites theological reflection and can actually make new things happen.

Two other feasts derive from a later post-exile context. The book of Esther describes the roots of the feast of Purim (see Chapter 7 below), a feast that celebrates Jewish identity and its persistence despite persecution and disadvantage. The feast of Hanukkah celebrates the rededication of the Temple after its defilement by Gentiles in the second century BC. The origins of this festival can be found in 1 Maccabees 4.36–59, after the successful conclusion of the Maccabean wars. The first act of the victors was to cleanse the Temple and refurbish it, then relight the Temple lights. These two feasts relating to the maintenance of Jewish identity are still celebrated today with new customs. For example, Purim is celebrated in a carnival atmosphere and there are competitions to see how quickly the book of Esther, with its tongue-twisting names, can be read. Hanukkah has attracted a number of domestic features, including the use of special toys. This festival includes the rubric, 'They were to observe [these days] as days of feasting and joy, days for sending presents of food to one another and gifts to the poor' (Esther 9.22). Brueggemann notes how attentiveness to the neighbour is one of the practices that are pivotal in Israel's worship (Brueggemann, 2002, p. 237). Edith can make real connections here, thinking of Harvest Festival as a time in her own church when there is opportunity to demonstrate generosity and sharing either of harvest gifts or their monetary equivalent.

There are two other practices in Brueggemann's list that we have not mentioned specifically. They are 'the *vigorous, disciplined remembering* of YHWH's "mighty deeds," most often a memory of YHWH's goodness (as in Pss. 105, 136)' and '*vigorous imagination about the future*' (2002, p. 237; emphasis in original).

TO DO

Imagine yourself in Edith's position as a worship leader and decide if and how any of these rituals and feasts has modern application. Think specifically about dealing with sin, acknowledging gifts from God, accepting stewardship, responsibility to the poor and alien (you might ask just who that is today), and maintaining good and right relations with a creator God, while holding a vision for the future.

Scholars note that the Exile must have had a profound effect on Israel's worship. The rebuilt Temple in Jerusalem could by no means have been a simple reflection of its predecessor. Gerstenberger, for instance, observes: 'the temple now worked for the confessing community of Israel, and no longer for the Davidic dynasty, and the preservation of the state, its military and officials' (Gerstenberger, 2002, p. 253). The 'established church' had become just one symbol of national identity. Alongside this we see some evidence of a reinterpretation of ancient community sacrificial rites in terms of individual ethical requirements. Isaiah 58 is a good example. Psalm 51.16f. maintains the same theme. Moreover the opportunities for communal gathering in the Dispersion are far more limited, and some way has to be found to give voice to individual, isolated piety. Daniel 6.10 describes how Daniel, an exile, prays facing Jerusalem three times a day 'as was his custom'.

There is one other aspect of Edith's question that she thinks might be important, and that is how the early Christian community itself used the Old Testament traditions in its own distinctive worship.

A complete description of worship from a New Testament perspective is clearly beyond our brief, but a few general comments may be made. There are no resources in the New Testament that correspond to the Psalms, or the descriptions of festivals and rituals that make up the bulk of Old Testament resources, for a discussion on this subject. Colossians 3.16 mentions singing psalms and hymns and spiritual songs but there are few possible examples, and those that have been identified as possibilities are deeply embedded in texts (such as 1 Corinthians 13). Some scholars have seen the outline of liturgies in 1 Peter and Revelation, and there do appear to be some liturgical fragments in both books; but the most interesting thing that can be said, and which bears any relation to our discussion to date, is that both those books have a deep interest in suffering, and the correspondence might be noticeable on that account. The Gospels give an account of the Last Supper, which formed part of later liturgies, and there is Gospel teaching on prayer and holiness in the great sermon (Matthew 5.23f.; 6.1–13, 16–18).

But there is evidence that the early Church appropriated what it considered to be foundational identifying symbols of classical Israel and applied them for its own use. The Temple and sacrificial system is completely re-imagined in 1 Peter 2.4–10. The new temple theme is also important in Revelation. The eucharistic tradition can be interpreted as the messianic feast (Isaiah 25.6–8), based among other evidence on its importance in the Wedding Feast of the Lamb in Revelation (Revelation 21.9–22). Jesus is portrayed as a successor to the Old Testament high priest at Hebrews 9.11, in a book whose apologetic strategy is based on reinterpreting Old Testament sacrificial practice and theology. Other links are less obvious. The necessity of communal worship might be regarded as one of them (see Hebrews 10.25 for an exhortation to attend meetings). Acts 2.11 sets an agenda for the early Church in terms of telling the mighty acts of God.

TO DO

Can you add to this brief list anything you have found in the Old Testament that resonates either with something from the New Testament or indeed from your own experience of church worship today? Do you know Edith?

As to Edith's original question: there is certainly much in the Old Testament that would resource any liturgical occasion when creation theology were predominant. Occasions of thanksgiving, dependence, stewardship and communal celebration of life-events might provide examples. Certainly there are resources for the suffering, based on the lament, and for those trying to find words to describe their vision of an ideal future. The Old Testament in fact provides much more evidence of worshipping communities and data about them than does the New Testament. The New Testament gives the clues as to how specifically Christian belief can be accommodated in Old Testament models.

Further reading

Brueggemann, W., 2014, *From Whom No Secrets Are Hid: Introducing the Psalms,* Louisville, KY: Westminster John Knox Press.

Holdsworth, J., 2010, *Lies, Sex and Politicians: Communicating the Old Testament in Contemporary Culture,* London: SCM Press.

Von Rad, G., 1966, *Deuteronomy: A Commentary,* London: SCM Press.

Westermann, C., 1981, *Praise and Lament in the Psalms* (trans. K. R. Crim and R. N. Soulen), Atlanta, GA: John Knox Press.

7

Is there any point in reading Chronicles, Ezra and Nehemiah?

There was a time when Gary had considered ordination. In the end he had settled for becoming a journalist, but maintained a well-informed interest in Bible texts. Part of his decision not to pursue ordination had resulted from his awareness of being gay, and now he is happily established in a civil partnership with his long-term partner Terry. Gary had never really been able to come to terms with what the Old Testament had to say about purity, which seemed so much at odds with New Testament teaching and so negative from his perspective. Some of that was in books like Leviticus, often quoted by those opposed to same-sex relationships, but Gary is also aware of a different seam of material, seldom noticed by Christians, namely the books of Chronicles, Ezra and Nehemiah. These seemed to set out a blueprint for religion as pure in the sense of 'alike' and 'exclusive'. These texts are troubling to him in his present situation as one who wants to be welcomed into a church that is an inclusive alternative community, and he sees them as real barriers to faith and evangelism in his own times. For him they 'get in the way'. So his question is: 'Is there any point in reading Chronicles, Ezra and Nehemiah?'

Two of the books that Gary has identified, Ezra and Nehemiah, provide the only narrative account of the period during which most of the rest of the Old Testament was being formed into material for publication. Theologically they appear related to both Chronicles and other writings that we have identified from the P perspective, such as Leviticus and Genesis 1. They are therefore important in providing a context in which to consider the competing theologies that result from the Exile. They themselves, of course, do not provide a 'neutral' or disinterested account. They are propagandist, and have a point to make. In English-language Bibles, Chronicles, Ezra and Nehemiah follow on from the history as told by the Deuteronomistic perspective – also propagandist – found in the books of Joshua through to 2 Kings. Following what appears to be the narrative strand, Chronicles precedes Ezra and Nehemiah. In Hebrew Bibles the D history (Joshua—2 Kings) is part of the Prophets section of the Scriptures (the Former Prophets in fact), and Chronicles, Ezra and Nehemiah are in the Writings section, so their separation is more apparent. Their order there is different too, with Chronicles following the other two to become the last book of the Hebrew Scriptures. Thus in Hebrew Bibles the Old Testament does not end in the way most Western Christians have come to accept: with the pregnant pause before the coming of the expected Messiah. Rather it ends with the hope of a new beginning for the remnant community of YHWH in Jerusalem, vouched for by King Cyrus of Persia with the rallying call: 'Whoever among you belongs to his people, may the LORD his God be with him, and let him go up [to Jerusalem]' (2 Chronicles 36.23).

Until the sixteenth century Chronicles and Ezra—Nehemiah were treated, respectively, as just one book rather than two (Ryle, 1909, p. 246). Ezra—Nehemiah appears to follow from where Chronicles ends, and for a long time there was a widespread acceptance of the face value assessment that one author or group of authors was responsible for all three, which were seen as one project (e.g. Schofield, 1969). However, there is a consensus in recent scholarship (e.g. Williamson, 1985; Brettler, 1995; Klein, 2001) that that is unlikely to be the case, although there are ideological similarities since they deal with common themes.

Ezra and Nehemiah are not easy reads, and one can see Gary's point in wondering why we might make the effort. There are various long lists of different categories of people, interspersed with official documents from various kings and governors, portions of prayer and liturgy as well as narrative. This provides an absolute gold mine for the source critic. Williamson (1987) devotes almost half his Old Testament guide for Ezra and Nehemiah to the question of their sources, without which, he claims, proper exegesis is impossible. Of particular interest in Nehemiah are those passages written in the first person. This so-called memoir of Nehemiah includes chapters 1—2, 4—6, 7.1–5, 12.31–43, 13.4–31, and reveals what Brueggemann calls 'a self-glorifying entrepreneur' (2003, p. 363). The whole account describes initial returns by the exiles from Babylon; initial attempts to rebuild the Temple and the walls; the first celebration of the Passover; the reading of the law that from now on will constitute the foundation document for true Jews; and the enactment of the Covenant that will bind them to it. Scholars do regard the historic outline as realistic. The return of Ezra is usually dated around 458, and that of Nehemiah 444.

The contents of Ezra and Nehemiah fall into well-marked sections. Ezra 1—6 deals with the initial return from exile to Jerusalem. Chapters 7—10 describe the leadership of Ezra. Nehemiah has a first-person narrative base but 8—10 are particularly important. Chapter 8 is the proclamation of the law to the people (the scholarly consensus is that this probably equates to our Pentateuch), and chapter 9 describes their response, in the form of a rehearsal of the history of Israel presented as a prayer. The whole occasion is given the context of feast and rejoicing. Notable is the final section of the descriptive prayer in which the people are described as being in dire distress. Today we are slaves, they say, in the land you gave to our forefathers (Nehemiah 9.36f.). This is in marked contrast to the generally positive relationship to the Persian kings that the rest of the books seem anxious to present. That may point to the tension the community is aware of and its new vulnerability within a puppet regime. It may also point towards tension within the community about whether it is right to accept the status quo and work within it or that an eschatological hope for the restoration of the Davidic line should have precedence, so making explicit that the present time is an interim period of convenience and compromise (see Williamson, 1987, p. 87).

> ## TO DO
>
> Think about the position of the religious community here, totally dependent on the goodwill of the political powers yet anxious to establish a religious integrity and identity. Think of the options available to them. Can you think of situations in the world today where the Christian Church exists in a similar setting? Should the Church be 'underground' and separate, or should it work with the state so long as there is common purpose? Share your thoughts.

Gary's question draws attention to some of the key issues in Ezra and Nehemiah that deal with purity and exclusion. The first of these issues poses the question: 'Who are real Jews? Is it those who have remained in the land or is it the returnees?' The task of rebuilding is jealously guarded by the returnees (strangely). Attempts to help from those who had remained in the land (Ezra 4.2f.) are rebuffed (4.3, 21), with the suggestion that these people's purity cannot be guaranteed. A whole chapter (Ezra 2) is devoted to establishing what one commentator calls the 'pedigrees of purity' of those who return (Brueggemann, 2003, p. 365).

The second concerns the matter of mixed marriages. Ezra 9 includes a long reflection on how the 'holy seed' (a characteristic phrase) of Israel has been polluted. God is reported as having forbidden marriages with foreigners:

> do not marry your daughters to their sons or take their daughters for your sons; nor must you ever seek their welfare or prosperity. Only thus will you be strong and enjoy the good things of the land, and hand it on as an everlasting possession to your descendants. (9.12)

This contrasts sharply with Jeremiah's prophecy to the exiles: 'marry wives and rear families ... Seek the welfare of any city to which I have exiled you' (Jeremiah 29.4–9). Nehemiah 13.23–27 takes up the same separatist theme. But the events outlined in Ezra 10 are perhaps the most shocking. It is decided to dismiss all the foreign wives and their children in an act of mass divorce, in order to maintain purity. The fact that a 'system' for arranging the dismissal is put in place is, in a sense, even more chilling.

TO DO

Read Ezra 10. With what historic events of the past hundred years or so could you compare this action? What might you say to Ezra from your experience of subsequent history? What do you think his reply might be?

The actions of Ezra and Nehemiah are not only legitimized by their claim to purity and their enlistment only of those who are pure in their view (Ezra 16.16f.), but also by the secular power of the Persian rulers (Ezra 4.3; 6.6ff.; 7.11ff.; Nehemiah 1.8f.). This sense of subjection to Persian power is carefully presented as a positive and protective and legitimizing thing, but occasionally there is a hint of a different view. Ezra 9.7 acknowledges the historic reality of subjection: 9.9 goes so far as to describe the plight of the people and their own priests and rulers as one of slavery, yet clearly there is a desire to see the hand of God at work in a more discreet way (cf. the theme of the book of Esther, also dealing with the plight of Jews under foreign domination – see below). Gary does accept that his questions come from a very different political and religious setting from those presupposed in the books in question. He can identify different dilemmas and sympathize to that extent, but these introductory comments do perhaps show us that if we are to understand what motivated the writers of Chronicles and Ezra—Nehemiah, we probably need to start from a different perspective from that suggested by Gary's question and concern, and to think rather about questions of the crisis of the Exile and identity.

TO DO

If you visit The Museum of the Jewish People (*Beit Hatfutsot*) in Tel Aviv, one of the first questions posed and answered is: 'How have the Jews managed to maintain their identity throughout the centuries when they have had no sovereign state and have been scattered throughout the countries of the world?' The answer is contained in the symbols of synagogue, bathhouse, butchers and family table.

Christians are also spread throughout the world. What do you think are the essential symbols of their identity?

We might begin by asking why two quite involved histories were written at all. The one that we have called the D history, which is associated with the radical school of 'second-law' writers and thinkers, with royal patronage from King Josiah, was the first to be published. The ordering and verbal similarities suggest that the author (or authors) of Chronicles, the second history, had the D history (the books from Joshua to 2 Kings) in front of him (or them as the case may be) as the new history was written (though this timeline has been challenged by Auld (1994) in his *Kings Without Privilege*). The answer is probably to be found in the experience of the Exile itself. As we have seen, that experience prompted a crisis for faith. For people who had believed in YHWH on the basis of a promise of land, of progeny and of a special relationship, the Exile promised to be a negation of all three. The first question for people of faith was therefore: 'Where is God in all this? How could God let this happen?'

As people who wanted to continue in faith, rather than simply give up, the D writers felt that there must be an answer to those questions and that the history of the nation might contain them. However, it is a little more complicated than that. These writers came to the questions with the answer ready to hand. It was the message they had been preaching long before the crisis struck. Tragedy had happened not because of inconsistency within the purposes of God, rather it was all the people's fault. They had been careless of the relationship and failed to keep their side of the covenant agreement. But even more culpable than the mass of the people were their leaders. Israel had been badly led, with few exceptions (one of which was of course King Josiah). The history story they tell, therefore, is designed to illustrate their argument. The narrative dwells on the faults and weaknesses of kings – none more so than the Davidic line. The so-called succession narrative within the D history (2 Samuel 11—1 Kings 2) describes adultery, abuse, murder, rape, incest and fratricide that would make the most dysfunctional soap-opera family look normal, and all in a racy tabloid newspaper style.

The D histories follow on from the book of Deuteronomy itself, which might properly be seen as the constitutive document for the D movement. This book describes a positive message of, and call for, reform. Set at the point where entry to the land is imminent, chapter 28 gives a glimpse into the future.

> If they abide by the teaching in Deuteronomy they will have blessing in the land, but if they worship other gods they will be cursed. The text dwells on the sufferings such a curse would entail, as though the writer already knows that disaster has befallen Israel. (Mills, 1999, p. 7)

In other words, the suggestion is that this is a retrospective account. The authors believe in quality of religion and want to establish one centre for the worship of YHWH in Jerusalem. This is to reflect the one-ness of God and the uniqueness of the covenant relationship (see Gooder, 2000, p. 100). They are keen that the people have a strong sense of God's gifts, both of the land (Deuteronomy 9.4) and of the law (4.40), and the prophetic voice (13.1–5; 18.20–22). Rejoicing is a key theme (Deuteronomy 28.63; 30.9; 12.7; 14.26; 26.11), and ritual is seen as an opportunity for rejoicing (16.14). Hence the D writings can be seen as a combination of political commentary and theology (Mills, 1999, p. 98). The question of the identity of Israel, according to Mills, stems from its vocation: 'Israel is meant to be a witness to God's own character, by its faithfulness in mirroring divine intentions through its maintenance of a proper social system' (Mills, 1999, p. 104).

The Chroniclers' history also deals with questions of 'what went wrong' and of identity but reaches conclusions that have a different practical outcome. The theological issue they faced was still to do with why the Exile had happened but it was also to do with the present perceived distance or even absence of God. The P writers developed what we have called a sacramental kind of theology to deal with the latter issue. This built on to creation theology a new realization of the sacredness of the land and of creation altogether. The reason the Exile had happened was somehow to do with the defiling of the land, which in turn meant not observing the proper boundaries put in place carefully in creation.

The treatment of purity issues in Leviticus may be seen in this light. The anthropologist Mary Douglas has written extensively on this subject (originally Douglas, 1966). She describes uncleanness as 'matter out of place' (p. 41). There are three kinds of creatures described in Genesis 1, which can be characterized as having, severally, wings, fins and feet. 'Any class of creatures which is not equipped for the right kind of locomotion in its element is contrary to holiness' (p. 57, quoted by Gooder, 2000, p. 98). Gooder relates this to the belief in the one-ness of God, and notes Douglas's conclusion that purity laws are not meant to maintain a status quo, as is normally the case in ancient societies, but rather to remind Israelites of their obligation towards holiness in a wider sphere. 'In Israel their concern was not so much politics as justice' (Gooder, 2000, p. 98).

Certainly, Genesis 1 is the basis of all P theology, and that is reflected in Chronicles, which begins its historical account with Adam rather than with a historical narrative already in process. The practical issues were addressed from the standpoint of the experience of what had sustained this community during its Exile and what had enabled it to keep its identity. Since Chronicles follows closely the structure of the D history, it is relatively easy to see where the two diverge and to build a picture of the distinctive characteristics of each in a redaction-critical kind of way. The differing degrees

of respect for the Davidic institutions, for example, are well illustrated by comparing 2 Samuel 11 to 1 Chronicles 20.

TO DO

Compare the two passages 2 Chronicles 34.1—35.26 and 2
Kings 22.1—23.25. What differences do you see? How do you
account for them? How might your findings help you interpret
the books?

The Hebrew title of Chronicles is 'The Events of the Days', which has
a rather more dynamic feel to it than its usual English title. An organized reading might find four sections. The first section, 1 Chronicles
1—9, is an extended genealogy setting out an ambitious aim to tell
a history of the world. Chapter 6 is worthy of note as it describes
the special role of the Levites, which is a distinctive trait. The second
section, chapters 11—29, tells the story of David, in which the preparations for the Jerusalem Temple, chapters 22—26, seem to have a
disproportionate place. A possible explanation is that 'the story of
David revolves around the establishment of legitimate cultic practice' (Brueggemann, 2003, p. 378). The third section, 2 Chronicles
1—9, describes Solomon, particularly in his role as temple builder.
In this account he is not subject to the negative comment of the D
histories (1 Kings 11.1–9). The final section is 2 Chronicles 10.1—
36.23, which covers the period from Rehoboam to the events of the
Exile. This differs from its D counterpart in its disregard for northern
kings. There is little mention of Elijah and Elisha (only at 21.12) who,
of course, have a major role in the D history. Other significant differences include the rubbishing of Saul in a very dismissive fashion
(1 Chronicles 10.13f.), with no real account of the rise of David.
Also there is no comparable passage to 1 Chronicles 13.1–4, where
the establishment of Jerusalem as the cult centre is agreed by 'the
whole nation' (13.4). The differing accounts of who was responsible for the hated census of Israel – YHWH (2 Samuel 24.1) or Satan
(1 Chronicles 21.1) – are also illuminating.

While we can see differences between the two histories, then, and can appreciate the reasons why they may differ, that does not really answer the question as to why both appear in the Scriptures. John Jarick (2002) believes that this was an embarrassment for the author(s) of Chronicles. His view is that Chronicles was meant to supersede any rival narratives and to be the constitutive history of the people, but that the canonical compilers had other ideas. We might see this as maintaining a principle that one set of traditions and beliefs do not 'trump' another, throughout the Old Testament, as we have already seen in Genesis 1—11, but that alternative responses to questions raised are allowed to stand side by side.

The theological themes common to these books are to do with continuity and identity. The continuity question has two parts. One concerns God: is the present time a continuation of the salvation history of the past? The other concerns the people: are these people in every respect the successors of the pre-exile Israel community? According to Williamson, 'continuity and purpose at the level of divine causality receive a heavy emphasis' (1987, p. 79). The history is not told as a historian would tell it. For example, there is a 50-year gap in the 'after these events' of Ezra 7.1. That would be unacceptable in secular history but is quite legitimate in salvation history. The lines of connection with the pre-exile community are drawn through the continuation of institutions, such as the Temple and its personnel, through genealogical purity (hence its importance) and through the concept of return to the land itself, particularly as Exodus imagery is used to describe it (e.g. Ezra 1.11; cf. Exodus 33.1).

All this tells us that there are a number of contemporary parallels between the situation faced after the Exile and the situations of some Christians today. It also gives a helpful insight into the folk memory of modern Jews. It outlines one option for those faced with the demise of their religion and describes a kind of revival. It describes how, and more importantly why, Judaism became the religion of the book and how that had repercussions for the practice of religion criticized by Jesus himself. But it actually makes no contribution at all to Gary's question, prompted as it is by concerns about sexuality that have no bearing on the context of the texts in question.

> **TO DO**
>
> From your reading so far, how would you answer Gary's question, and what might you say to him about the way the OT is sometimes used in modern ethical debates?

There is one further book, not mentioned by Gary, but one that gives an important insight into the post-exile community (not this time centred in Jerusalem but scattered throughout the eastern Mediterranean), and that is the book of Esther, which is placed in Greek and English Bibles immediately after Ezra and Nehemiah. This was not its original place, but its being placed here suggests that editors recognized the usefulness of grouping these three books. Originally it was in the Writings section of the Hebrew Scriptures as one of the five scrolls or Megilloth that are set to be read at specific Jewish festivals. The others are Ruth, Song of Songs, Ecclesiastes, and Lamentations. Esther is set for Purim, the carnival feast that has come to celebrate the victory of Jewishness over its detractors and enemies.

Theologically there are similarities between Esther and Lamentations. Both express the absence of God. In Lamentations this is partial. We long for God's voice but never hear it. Nevertheless, God is named and faith in God is expressed. In Esther, God is never named, mentioned or yearned for. In fact it could be said that the main themes of the book are exactly the absence of God, God's lack of interest in the people in a foreign land and God's disinclination to intervene in their plight. Christians have found a variety of ways of reading the book. One is to see it as providing a further insight into the issues of particularity affecting dispersed Jews. Others have placed it alongside other mini-novels, such as the first part of the book of Daniel and the stories of Joseph in Genesis, as providing inspiration for how Jews should behave in foreign cultures in a way that offers the prospect of public participation – despite the dangers and snares – while maintaining specific faith and identity. Miles (1995) concentrates on how this story, with its absence of

God, fits a biography of God. Beckett (2002) attempts a Christo-logical exegesis that involves seeing Esther as a type of Jesus (p. 7). Brueggemann (2003) approaches the book from the perspective of the festival it supports, and describes it as, 'a huge act of subversive, dissenting imagination' (p. 348).

TO DO

Read the book of Esther. It is one of the few true page-turners in the Old Testament and you should find it entertaining. Do any of the approaches mentioned above appeal to you? Why do you think that the author fails to mention God? Is it:

- Just an accident – he takes God so much for granted that he doesn't have to mention him?
- Because he is an atheist who believes that belief in God has had its day, and it is now time for humans to live by their instincts and wiles?
- Because he wants to reassure readers that, although God seems absent, God is really working behind the scenes to procure a good outcome for the Jews?
- Because he wants to warn Jews of the ever-present threat of discrimination that is not simply religious?
- Because he wants to find a new non-religious basis for national celebration?

Or is there some other reason? Share your conclusions with the group.

The story, briefly, concerns a sequence of events in the Persian empire. The king throws a great feast lasting seven days and, when thoroughly inebriated, calls for the queen, Vashti, to come and do a turn in front of the assembled men. She, of course, refuses. This causes a crisis, and is generally regarded as a dangerous precedent. Consequently Vashti is banished and normality is resumed. Every man is master in his own house. Even in its own time this must have been seen as the prelude to some comic outcome, but first events take a darker turn. Prior to that, though, the king is without a queen, and so chapter 2 describes how he chooses a virgin to replace Vashti. The girl he chooses is Esther, a Jewess, who has been adopted by her older cousin, Mordecai. He has given her strict instructions not to disclose that she is a Jew. Almost as a footnote, though it is important later in the story, Esther and Mordecai foil a plot to assassinate the king.

The next stage is the appointment of Hamam as, effectively, prime minister. Mordecai offends him and he decides to use this opportunity as a final solution for the Jews, and persuades the king to allow their extermination. The king shows little interest (3.11) and Hamam is allowed to continue his plot against the Jews. Esther is informed of the plot and its author and is persuaded to petition the king on the Jews' behalf. Chapter 5 introduces Esther's counter-plot, though it is not clear to the reader how this will proceed. What we do see is that Hamam is preparing a gallows for Mordecai. Chapter 6 reprises the plot against the king that Mordecai had helped foil. The king remembered that Mordecai had not been properly thanked for his part in this, and in an ironic way Hamam, his enemy, was called upon to devise a reward. Hamam's wife's words are notable: 'If you have begun to fall before Mordecai and he is a Jew, you cannot get the better of him; your downfall before him is certain' (6.13). This prophecy proves correct. Following a scene of sheer farce, Hamam is hanged on the gallows he had himself prepared for Mordecai.

The remaining chapters make uneasy reading. First, Esther secures the cancellation of the king's decree against the Jews. So far so good. 'All was light and joy, gladness and honour for the Jews' (8.16). But the king's decree goes further and gives the Jews permission to kill anyone they considered to be an enemy. Chapter 9 becomes a catalogue of slaughter of hundreds of people without any comment on the disproportionate nature of a response to the plot of a single man. The feast of Purim is then inaugurated as a time to celebrate, share food and send gifts to the poor, and Mordecai takes the place of Hamam as prime minister – taking care to protect the interests of the Jews.

The answer to Gary's question, then, might be that there is a point in reading these books, but not the point he was looking for. These are not books describing right conduct in sexual relationships or exploring the limits of inclusiveness. They have to be read as books that deal with fundamental questions about religious identity, both in a benign state and in times of malign intent. They describe the narrow lines that have to be drawn that enable some public theology and participation and help avoid the descent into sectarianism, while maintaining a religious life with its own rules and values. They give insight into the real fears of the people that God is absent. They describe a response to those fears that in time leads to a practice of religion criticized by Jesus. They give insight into the mindset of some modern-day Jews and perhaps, at a different level, exemplify a way of describing a religious life without religious language.

Further reading

Alter, R., 1998, 'The Poetic and Wisdom Books', in J. Barton (ed.), *The Cambridge Companion to Biblical Interpretation*, Cambridge: Cambridge University Press, pp. 226–40.

Cary, P., 2008, *Jonah* (SCM Theological Commentaries), London: SCM Press.

Klein, R. W., 2001, 'Narrative Texts: Chronicles, Ezra and Nehemiah', in L. G. Perdue (ed.), *The Blackwell Companion to the Hebrew Bible*, Oxford: Blackwell, pp. 385–401.

Larkin, K. J. A., 1995, *Ruth and Esther* (Old Testament Guides), Sheffield: Sheffield Academic Press.

8

Does the Old Testament have anything to say about being a good person?

Sarah was brought up in a family that went to church reasonably frequently. She herself went to Sunday school. She remembered little of what had been taught but had vivid and warm memories of those who taught her. Now, as a mother of two small children herself, she wants them to go to Sunday school too and have the immersion in church culture she had. Her husband has no such memory and is sceptical about the whole thing, and so Sarah finds herself having to defend a decision she feels instinctively is right. She frames her argument in terms of the children learning values and having good moral examples to follow. Indeed, for many of the adults she has known through her church contact, this is actually the reason they go to church at all – to learn how to be better people, she says.

Her husband responds that, on the contrary, the Old Testament in particular, as he has dipped into it, appears to contain many bad examples and is not a particularly good moral guide at all. The questions this response raises for Sarah extend beyond the family. She is a primary school head teacher and encourages a Bible-based assembly for her school, often referring to the Old Testament for its story element. If parents question this, she defends her decision in the same way she has to her husband. A broadly Christian assembly can be Bible-based as it teaches values and helps children to understand moral choices. But the criticisms have stuck and now Sarah seeks reassurance: 'Does the Old Testament have anything to say about being a good person?'

TO DO

At this point it might be useful to reflect on how central ethics is as a theme of the Old Testament. To do this, try to devise a series of subtitles for the Old Testament, such as 'The Old Testament: A History of God and God's People' or 'The Old Testament: The Old Covenant'. In other words, try to sum up as succinctly as possible what, from your reading so far, you think the Old Testament is fundamentally about. Then see if any of your subtitles mentions or implies anything ethical. Compare answers and see if you can agree on a 'winner'.

The point of the exercise is to illustrate that essentially the Old Testament does not set out to be a textbook of ethics. Whatever it is thought to be about, it is not arranged as the kind of book that one might refer to to see what action were appropriately ethical in a given situation, though sections of it might once have been used in that way. It is certainly a series of texts about God, and that sets it apart from those ethical systems that start with humankind (how to achieve the greatest good for the greatest number, for example). Neither does it – as in Aristotelian ethics – start from the end and then debate the means. Whatever the Bible has to say about ethics starts with God and God's nature. We have already seen, in response to Gary's question, that there are dangers, in our own time, in approaching the texts with ethical questions deriving from a completely different culture and setting from those that prompted the text originally. There are also dangers in expecting to find in the Old Testament a unified system of ethics. Yet there are sections and ideas important to ethical debate. First, if we were to devise a subtitle along the lines of, for example, 'The Old Testament: The Formation and Development of a Religious Identity', which on the face of it does not sound ethical as such, we would still find that identity issues are inevitably tied up with ethical issues. Defining 'the kind of people we are' – that is, defining distinctiveness – will almost certainly refer to ethical values. In the case of the Old Testament the identity of the people of Israel as those who could assent to the Covenant is a central part of their identity. Second, the covenant concept does make specific moral demands and, as Torah, is a point of reference. Third, each generation of Old Testament writers – and as such theologians – deals with and develops the concept of 'law'. Fourth, the distinctiveness of the Old Testament is sometimes still described in terms of 'ethical monotheism'. Fifth, the Old Testament contains many moral tales describing behaviour that is judged as displeasing to God.

As the Old Testament presents itself, we might see three 'cross cuts' that would provide ethical discussion. First is the Covenant itself; second is the use of the covenant idea in the prophets, and particularly the pre-exilic prophets; and third would be the re-expression of the law that we have seen in the post-exilic period following the return.

The Book of the Covenant, the name often given to Exodus 20—23, is the first intentional or formal statement of ethics we come across in the Old Testament. It represents the human response required by God to his initiative to form a relationship with human-kind that promises both progeny and territory. It contains much that is common to the culture of the area, as one might expect. It is usual to make a distinction between the words of God, which set out the fundamental axioms of what will become the law (apodictic law), and the development and application of those laws by human agency to particular situations (casuistic law). The first are uncondi-tional; the latter conditional.

If we compare this text with, for example, the Babylonian Codes of Hammurabi, we find here a stronger emphasis on neighbour and, generally, a more egalitarian approach. So there are no dis-tinctions between rich and poor. This is a constant Old Testament theme, reiterated in creation theology at, for instance, Proverbs 22.2. In Exodus, and particularly Deuteronomy (26.5–11; 8.12–18; 4.37–42), the motive against partiality is the common experience of being slaves in Egypt, which should breed both a sense of humility and of compassion for the poor and slaves. So slaves are not dealt with just as chattels and possessions. Their feelings are respected to a degree (Exodus 21.2–6, 7–11, 26f., 32). Also God's characteristic concern is seen to be for the weak and distressed, particularly for widows and orphans – again a characteristic biblical litany, which persists to New Testament times (James 1.27). Obligations towards the poor and distressed are seen as a matter of justice rather than charity.

Prophetic ethics is concerned with applying the lessons of what the prophets apparently believe to be a disregarded covenant to their present day. From the eighth century BC onwards, Israel becomes a far more sophisticated society in which the distance between rich and poor is far more pronounced and in which new questions about the moral duties of nations and not just individuals have relevance for the first time, as international trade and politics have developed. Amos reminds a nation – that apparently disagrees – that any successful society must have morality at its heart. He points to the evidence of corruption that he sees (Amos 2.6–8; 4.1; 5.7–13; 8.4–6). He asserts God's impartiality by including judgements against the nations alongside judgement on Israel (1.3—2.16) and invites them to judge themselves by the criteria they use to judge others. We can perhaps imagine a society in which religion is considered to be little more than a curiosity of cultural history with little reference to current realities and completely without power: certainly in which it has ceased to be a point of moral reference.

Amos has the most detailed description of the wrongs of corruption and oppression. We can get an idea here of the situation the Deuteronomists faced. Their concern was to relaunch the religion of YHWH with a new centre of excellence and a new statement of the law that paid attention to both the motivations for good behaviour and the consequences of bad. Some of the latter may have been retrospective but the movement was pre-exilic and closely affected by the message of the prophets. They put a new emphasis on education and the place of the home in maintaining and transmitting the law. Micah's summary of the demands of the Covenant for a new generation (Micah 6.8) is an adequate summary of the early prophetic message.

The exilic and post-exilic years bring a variety of new questions and approaches. Here we see the movement from a self-determined political society to a religious community. One consequence is the movement from a communal approach to a more individual one. Ezekiel 18 describes this movement well, as the prophet denies that sin can in some way be inherited. In the process he sets out some useful lists of what, in Ezekiel's time, a righteous life and an unrighteous life might look like.

TO DO

Read Ezekiel 18. Can you spot the ways the Exodus covenant demands have been augmented and developed? What conclusions would you draw from this?

Similar lists can be found in the prophetic literature in relation to questions about coming into the presence of the Lord. What is the right attitude for worship? To whom will God really listen? Isaiah 1.12–17, Amos 5.21–24, Jeremiah 7.1–15 as well as the Micah passage all place their understanding of the Covenant in this context. It is interesting to read Psalm 15 alongside these prophetic utterances. It may be that there is a liturgical setting for such utterances.

The Wisdom literature, and particularly the book of Proverbs, offers some insights into domestic ethics from the perspective of the writers. Using the device of giving advice and teaching to the young, the author sets out a view of life that is echoed in Job 31. Proverbs gives a coherent picture of what is to be avoided in order to attain wisdom and life. The list includes adulteresses and prostitutes (Proverbs 6.32–35; 7.4–27; 23.26–28; 30.20), drunkenness (23.29–35), idleness (6.10f.), gossip (18.8) and bad judgement in the choice of a wife (25.24; 27.15f.). In general egocentricity is not seen as at odds with spiritual devotion and hedonism has a kind of divine sanction in that health, long life and material success are seen as the rewards of having cooperated with God's will. Solomon's wealth is evidence of his wisdom. This is, of course, the view challenged by the book of Job and by subversive commentary elsewhere (e.g. 1 Kings 10). If we were to ask what section of society would most benefit by adherence to these moral precepts, then we would use words like male, propertied, conservative, family orientated, but from a male perspective that looks for respect towards elders and sees the family as a context in which to maintain and exercise power.

As we have noticed, the post-exilic period sees people grappling with the issue of divine justice. The book of Job and the second section of the prophet Isaiah (40—55) both deal with this. This issue too has liturgical expression in the Psalms (e.g. Psalm 74). The question raised is why good people are not automatically rewarded for being good, neither are the bad punished. This is a fundamental ethical question that only really enters the fray with the advent and popularity of creation theology. With an increasingly international outlook new questions in the same mode arise, such as whether victorious nations are more righteous than those they conquer. This is the question reflected upon by the prophet Habakkuk, as well as, for example, Isaiah 10.5–19. The rise of post-exilic apocalyptic draws attention to the existence of evil in the world with a new intensity. The defeat of wickedness on a cosmic scale becomes a matter of ethical interest.

As we saw in Chapter 7 above, another movement in the post-exilic period is towards legalism, as Jews make a great stride in the direction of becoming the people of the book. But this is only the latest of a series of revised codes and legal formulations, which could be said to have started with the Deuteronomists and includes the Holiness code of Leviticus 17—26. In this period and culture we see the rise of ritual in worship, a concentration on external observance and more reference to God's acting in the past than in the present. The morally dubious aspects of legalism are, of course, highlighted by Jesus.

Sarah finds all of this interesting but somehow incomplete. It does demonstrate that new theological understandings lead both to new ethical consequences and to new liturgical material with an ethical component. But that just leaves a jumble of the views of interested parties with little connecting commentary. Also she has learned not to accept at face value the way the Bible presents its own story but to see beneath the veneer of that, so she finds the descriptions of ethics thus far rather flat and one-dimensional: disconnected from new critical insights. What she wants is the confidence to use Old Testament tools as a part of ethical enquiry in the present and in her own situation. While she may not want to introduce sophisticated layers of meaning into Old Testament narratives in an assembly setting, she would like to have a way of assuring herself that it is legitimate to use them.

TO DO

Read Leviticus 19. This contains (v. 18) one of the most persistent of ethical claims in the Judeo-Christian tradition. It is quoted by Jesus himself and by other New Testament writers (Mark 12.31; Luke 10.27; James 2.8). The question the lawyer puts to Jesus is one that naturally arises from the passage. Using if possible more than one translation, see how many kinds of people are described in Leviticus 19 as a whole ('poor', 'alien', 'kinsman' etc.). Then try to decide whether 'neighbour' is just one more in that group with a specific definition or whether it is the generic term for all of them. What do the categories have in common? And what is the strength of the word 'love'? Is it diminished by being widened? What difference does it make to your understanding of the passage to know that this comes from the P tradition, a tradition in which boundaries are very important, but also one in which right relationships are important; and that it may well be post-exilic?

One modern writer who would agree with Sarah is Daniel Smith-Christopher (2007). For someone whose avowed intent is to make the Bible accessible, it is perhaps unfortunate that the title of his recent work, *Jonah, Jesus, and Other Good Coyotes*, is intelligible only to Americans. The good coyotes of the title are people who help Mexicans cross the border into the USA, illegally but not cynically; that is, they do not take lots of money from them and then abandon them but rather make sure their border crossing is properly completed and the refugees are safe on the other side. They do this from motives that relate to justice and peace. This then acts as a model for what Smith-Christopher sees as the characteristic ethical behaviour of boundary crossing. The book is primarily about justice and peacemaking but it has important things to say about how we read the Bible and particularly the Old Testament, from the point of view of a scholar who has made a special study of the importance of the Exile in Old Testament writing.

He contrasts the Old Testament view of justice with that current in his own culture. He claims that demands for justice from individuals in the USA are often thinly veiled but socially acceptable demands for vengeance (2007, p. 3). Justice in the Old Testament view is not about personal satisfaction that evil has been punished but about wanting the best for the most disadvantaged: most notably, the widow, the orphan and the foreigner (Isaiah 1.17; Jeremiah 22.3; Ezekiel 22.7; Zechariah 7.10; Malachi 3.5). Moreover this majority prophetic voice is particularly critical of those whose responsibility it is to uphold and proclaim justice; that is, the religious establishment (Amos 5.21–24; Isaiah 10.1f.; Micah 3.1–4, 9–11).

He believes that the focus on the ten words of Exodus 20 has diverted attention from other important Mosaic law imperatives that fill out the Old Testament concept of justice. He cites the law of Jubilee (Leviticus 25). He refers to a bunch of laws found in Deuteronomy 24 and 25, dealing with the wages of the poor, the right to glean, punishment that is not degrading, the right of refuge for economic slaves, along with health and safety issues (placing railings on upper floors) and, intriguingly, what he claims is the expectation (Deuteronomy 20) that soldiers must have experienced the blessings of peace before becoming warriors (Smith-Christopher, 2007, pp. 13–20).

TO DO

Read Deuteronomy 20. Do you agree that the three exemptions from military service – planting a garden, building a house, being engaged to be married – are the basic signs of stable life? What conclusions do you draw from this? Does the passage offer any new or interesting insights into the Mosaic law?

Smith-Christopher's studies on the Exile and its theological consequences lead him to identify two different reactions to the captors. One is the angry demand for vengeance, as exemplified in such well-known Psalms as 137. But the other less celebrated voice is that which looks for the transformation of the enemy. He sees this as a central theme of 2 Isaiah (and those parts of 2 Isaiah he believes have become embedded in 1 Isaiah). Quoting Isaiah 49.6f.; 2.4f.; 19.20–25 and the tradition represented in Jeremiah 29.4–9 (which has those same three criteria of settled life), he makes the case for an alternative peacemaking voice, as one theological strand contributing to the underlying question: 'What does it mean to be the people of God now?'

The book of Jonah is further evidence, for him, of the necessity of border crossing. He also sees the story of Ruth as a counterpoint to the kind of thinking we see in Ezra 9, which describes the abandonment of foreign wives. Ruth is from Moab and yet is an antecedent of King David (and as Matthew 1.5 tells it, also of Jesus). He notes the links between P theology and peacemaking, contrasting the account in Genesis 1, for example, with the violent combat myths of surrounding cultures (2007, pp. 93ff.).

His writing deals, in passing, with two theological issues that have importance in the development, presentation and adaptation of ethical thought and that both have importance in recent scholarship. Both are evidenced in the book of Proverbs. Proverbs 30.24–28 is a poetic description of four kinds of animal. Smith-Christopher points out that 'in each case, the animals represent the condition of the Hebrew people after 587 BCE' (2007, p. 34). The animals in question are ants that are without strength, rock badgers that are without power, locusts that have no king and lizards that are small but evidenced all over the place, even in royal palaces. He concludes, 'This passage raises a central question (some may argue *the* central question) of post-587 BCE biblical thought: just what does it mean to be the people of God *now*?' (p. 34; emphasis in original). We have already seen how Ezra and Nehemiah dealt with this. What is interesting is to find this contextual remark in a book (Proverbs) that is dealing with right behaviour. We might observe that when all the 'protections' and power of institutions and privilege are removed and when the boundaries they imply have been demolished, the one thing left to mark out distinctiveness is behaviour, informed by attitudes and values. This is precisely the kind of conclusion Sarah would find useful as she seeks justification for a Bible-based school assembly.

We see something similar in the New Testament in 1 Peter. This Epistle is addressed interestingly also to exiles and to people at the bottom of the social ladder: people who are weak and powerless. No letter of the New Testament places more emphasis on the power of example and forbearance (1 Peter 2.12–15, 18f., 20–23; 3.8, 13–17; 4.7–11, 14–16; 5.5–7). Ezra and Nehemiah seek to enshrine somehow appropriate attitudes in a new law and address that to the new community. In the process they set up new barriers. Proverbs reflects the move towards personal responsibility and addresses the same issue in terms of the rather more intimate man-to-man conversations of the book. They exemplify two approaches in which ethical issues are central.

The other development noted by Smith-Christopher is the appearance of the new creation theology (2007, pp. 89ff.). He develops his argument, which is basically that P theology is a peaceful theology, by reference to the book of Genesis, but actually Proverbs is itself a product of creation theology. Creation theology is that view of God's relation with the world that springs from the realization that there is only one God and that the one God is a creator God. For the authors or editors of Proverbs, what that appears to mean is that if we want to know more about God's purposes for the world and God's intentions for humankind, we should observe God's creation closely. The creation reveals the will of the creator. So Proverbs engages in a kind of what we would now call social-scientific enquiry. As we have seen, it observes human behaviour and relations and sees what leads to tears (clearly therefore against God's will in creation) and what leads to fulfilment (obviously thereby cooperating with God's creative will).

Prior to creation theology the main reasons given for behaving well and in accord with God's will were related to God's act of liberation of the Hebrew slaves. Particularly in Deuteronomy the people are told to have a thankful attitude to life, to have due humility and true gratefulness. By extension that might also mean bringing the kind of freedom to others that they have enjoyed. The problem with creation theology is, as we have seen, that it can assume that what is the case is indeed what God intended; in other words, that creation is complete and good. However, that can never be the case while suffering exists. The response of creation theology – usually espoused by the comfortable and powerful who have a vested interest in the status quo – is charity; in other words, we should try to alleviate from within our means the results of (inevitable) suffering. The response of liberation/redemption theology is justice; that is, we should try to change the circumstances that bring about suffering, and that often means working for a realignment of power. These two theologies are central to the post-exilic debate, and both are still relevant more than 25 centuries later.

TO DO

Reflect together on Archbishop Hélder Câmara's words (Câmara was the Roman Catholic Bishop of Olinda and Recife in Brazil, a very poor diocese): 'When I give food to the poor they call me a saint. When I ask why they are poor, they call me a communist.'

Smith-Christopher is clearly up to speed with modern critical approaches. He sets a context for Old Testament discussion of ethics within the post-exilic theological melting pot of ideas that contribute to what it means to be a religious or holy people of God without a land or political entity, without a common language, without a common ethnicity or even without a common cultural heritage. He identifies justice as a dominant theme and relates that to his own interest in and commitment to peacemaking, in the context of the kind of despair that some US writers display when faced with the power of the 'religious right' in that country.

Another approach, based on recent scholarship, is exemplified by Mary Mills' study, *Biblical Morality* (Mills, 2001). Subtitled *Moral Perspectives in Old Testament Narratives,* and inspired by a short work by John Barton (1998b), the book seeks to explore what insights can be gained into Old Testament ethics from the movement in critical approaches, from those that favour the methods used by historians to those that favour the methods used by students of literature. Mills sees ethics operating at the level of personal relationships and values, societal relationships and values, and at a wider cosmic ontological level. She relates each of these in turn to a study, first, of character, using three biblical narratives: Abraham, David and Esther; then of plot, using the stories of Ruth, Joseph and Jonah. The cosmic perspective is illustrated by reference to Genesis 1—11, Daniel 1—7 and Job. She discovers a sophisticated intertwining of the perspectives in the narrative sections.

She concludes that the narrative sections of the Old Testament are a useful and intelligent medium for moral discourse, but it is a medium that involves the reader in making choices, which may be done either with the grain of the story or against it. For example, in the well-known story of David and Bathsheba some readers will concur with the grain of the story and hold David responsible for the subsequent misfortune because he knowingly committed adultery. Others will read against the grain and accuse Bathsheba of effectively asking for it by bathing naked in a place where she knew she might well be seen by a man. Again, the judgement that David's family is dysfunctional is essentially a judgement based on the concept of family from the twenty-first-century Western world. In the story of Ruth the reader may agree that Ruth is the heroine but may equally well take the part of Oprah who clings to tradition and boundary.

Narrative biography will inevitably describe complex beings with moral ambiguities. In narrative critical method, the reader plays a critical part in determining truth so it is unsurprising that Mills believes that 'the breadth of this interpretive process leads to an understanding that morality, in any given text, is not a single message, but consists of a plethora of interpretations, some contradictory to others' (Mills, 2001, p. 243). For her, that is not a disadvantage but merely the way ethical issues are approached by societies and individuals. The variety speaks of vitality rather than confusion. John Barton, whose John Albert Hall lectures inspired Mills' work, puts it thus:

> In the Old Testament we are presented, not with a carefully worked out code allegedly valid for all time, but with a way of handling life as it presented itself in all its brokenness and particularity in the societies which formed these texts as we now have them. (Barton, 1998b, p. 17)

For Sarah, this introduces a new responsibility as she recognizes that the texts that have an ethical component do not speak for themselves but rather need a 'readerly' interpretation.

The basic sentiments of these approaches are mirrored by Cyril Rodd (2001) in his collection of essays, *Glimpses of a Strange Land*. His choice of 'Glimpses' bears witness to his understanding of the variety of ethical material, and he illustrates the strangeness of the strange land by describing the strong links, unfamiliar to Western readers nowadays, between ethics and purity and ethics and honour, and the importance of custom within the community. A study of adultery leads to the conclusion that there may well be a large gap between the law as we read it and practical application, about which we have very few, and then inconsistent, glimpses. 'We shall probably never know how the man who seduced his neighbour's wife was actually treated, or what precise punishment was meted out to the wife who welcomed another man into her bed' (Rodd, 2001, p. 43). There is no account of anyone actually being put to death for adultery.

Rodd believes we can know very little about most Old Testament categories that have a bearing on ethics. For example, 'the king as Yahweh's representative clearly is an important figure in Old Testament ethics, yet the tensions between the ideal and the actual ... make it difficult to know how to relate the monarchy to ethics' (p. 300). Rodd believes that our contemporary interests can distort our interpretation of Old Testament ethics. 'To the Israelites the poor, war, the care of animals, dangers to the natural world and the position of women in society were not problems' (p. 159). It is in fact the very strangeness of the Old Testament world that we frequently disregard, which Rodd's book seeks to highlight. It is a readable and well-documented account from a self-confessed sceptical viewpoint, consistent with one main strand of Old Testament enquiry in the present.

TO DO

Read Deuteronomy 25.5–10. The result of failure to conform in this instance is not a juridical punishment but rather public shame. How do you respond to this? What part do you think shame should have or might have in the shaping of ethics?

Sarah has come to see that her view of the Old Testament as a source of ethical instruction was perhaps rather naïve. She has been fascinated to read parts of the Old Testament she hardly knew existed and to see the scope of the issue. She remains convinced that the Old Testament contains worthwhile ethical discussion but is more guarded about applying contemporary standards to the texts. She has found ways of organizing her reading of the ethical material, based on the Old Testament's own genres: law, liberation, creation theology, the role of the king, covenant and national and religious identity. She prefers the prescriptions of the New Testament but accepts that Old Testament people wanted to live a good life and spent as much time thinking about how to attain that as we do.

Further reading

Barton, J., 1998, *Ethics and the Old Testament*, London: SCM Press.

Brueggemann, W., 1994, *A Social Reading of the Old Testament* (ed. P. D. Miller), Minneapolis, MN: Fortress Press.

Kirsch, J., 1997, *The Harlot by the Side of the Road*, London: Rider Books.

Meyers, C., 2005, *Exodus* (The New Cambridge Bible Commentary), Cambridge: Cambridge University Press.

Mills, M. E., 1998, *Images of God in the Old Testament*, London: Cassell.

Wenham, G. J., 2000, *Story as Torah*, Edinburgh: T. & T. Clark.

Postscript:
What are you not telling me?

Recently I was part of a job interview panel. Eventually the process reached the point where the chairperson asked the candidate the inevitable 'Is there anything you'd like to ask us?' question. Following a moment's thought, he said, 'In a job description there's always something they don't tell you. What are you not telling me?' You may have a similar question having worked through this volume.

Let's begin by setting out what I hope you may be able to recognize in your own journey of adventure through the Old Testament. You should be able:

- to recognize the various genres of the Old Testament and to have strategies of organization for them;
- to distinguish between the story the writers want you to read and other subversive alternatives – in other words, to recognize reading strategies;
- through the provision of a manageable bibliography, to have confidence in accessing scholarship in relation to the Old Testament and have some tools for critical analysis of it;
- to speak about areas of the Old Testament in a way that engages with a non-specialist audience;
- to recognize links between the texts and contemporary experience that give strategies for that communicative task;
- to enjoy reading the Old Testament and to feel that you know what you are reading.

So what is left? Well, this book does not deal in detail with any particular book or theme in the Old Testament. It simply sets out to provide a more general map with a small scale, of the sort often found in the early pages of road atlases (in the olden days before satnav), telling you which page to go to for a more detailed look. Certainly if you are to make your journey interesting and get the most from it, you will need that larger scale. And if you want to get out of the car on the way and explore the paths of a particular hill, you will need a more detailed map still. This book is not designed to help you tick a box called 'Old Testament' on a 'must do' list. It is written to try to persuade you that it is worth getting hold of those other maps and making those other interesting journeys. As my son would say: it is what it is. I hope you enjoyed it.

Further reading

Barr, J., 1999, *The Concept of Biblical Theology: An Old Testament Perspective*, London: SCM Press.

Brown, M. J., 2000, *What They Don't Tell You: A Survivor's Guide to Biblical Studies*, Louisville, KY: Westminster John Knox Press.

References

Aciman, A., 1997, *Letters of Transit: Reflections on Exile, Identity, Language, and Loss*, New York: The New Press.

Albright, W. F., 1939, 'The Israelite Conquest of Canaan in the Light of Archaeology', *Bulletin of the American Schools of Oriental Research*, 74, pp. 11–22.

Alt, A., 1968, 'The Settlement of the Israelites in Palestine', in R. Wilson (ed.), *Essays on Old Testament History and Religion*, Garden City, NY: Doubleday, pp. 311–35.

Alter, R., 1982, *The Art of Biblical Narrative*, New York: Basic Books.

Alter, R., 1998, 'The Poetic and Wisdom Books', in J. Barton (ed.), *The Cambridge Companion to Biblical Interpretation*, Cambridge: Cambridge University Press, pp. 226–40.

Anderson, B. W., 1994, *From Creation to New Creation: Old Testament Perspectives*, Minneapolis, MN: Fortress Press.

Auld, A. G., 1994, *Kings Without Privilege: David and Moses in the Story of the Bible's Kings*, Edinburgh: T. & T. Clark.

Balentine, S. E., 2002, *Leviticus* (Interpretation Commentaries), Louisville, KY: John Knox Press.

Barr, J., 1999, *The Concept of Biblical Theology: An Old Testament Perspective*, London: SCM Press.

Barton, J., 1997, *Making the Christian Bible*, London: Darton, Longman & Todd.

Barton, J., 1998a (ed.), *The Cambridge Companion to Biblical Interpretation*, Cambridge: Cambridge University Press.

Barton, J., 1998b, *Ethics and the Old Testament*, London: SCM Press.

Beckett, M., 2002, *Gospel in Esther*, Carlisle: Paternoster Press.

Biggar, S. (ed.), 1989, *Creating the Old Testament: The Emergence of the Hebrew Bible*, Oxford: Blackwell.

Boesak, A. A., 1987, *Comfort and Protest: Reflections on the Apocalypse of John of Patmos*, Philadelphia, PA: Westminster Press.

Brettler, M. Z., 1995, *The Creation of History in Ancient Israel*, London: Routledge.

Bright, J., 1960, *A History of Israel*, London: SCM Press.

Brown, M. J., 2000, *What They Don't Tell You: A Survivor's Guide to Biblical Studies*, Louisville, KY: Westminster John Knox Press.

Brueggemann, W., 1982, *Genesis* (Interpretation Commentaries), Atlanta, GA: John Knox Press.

Brueggemann, W., 1984, *The Message of the Psalms: A Theological Commentary*, Minneapolis, MN: Augsburg Press.

Brueggemann, W., 1992, *Old Testament Theology: Essays on Structure, Theme, and Text*, Minneapolis, MN: Fortress Press.

Brueggemann, W., 1994, *A Social Reading of the Old Testament* (ed. P. D. Miller), Minneapolis, MN: Fortress Press.

Brueggemann, W., 1997, *Cadences of Home: Preaching Among Exiles*, Louisville, KY: Westminster John Knox Press.

Brueggemann, W., 1998, *A Commentary on Jeremiah*, Cambridge: Eerdmans.

Brueggemann, W., 2002, *Reverberations of Faith: A Theological Handbook of Old Testament Themes*, Louisville, KY: Westminster John Knox Press.

Brueggemann, W., 2003, *An Introduction to the Old Testament: The Canon and Christian Imagination*, Louisville, KY: Westminster John Knox Press.

Brueggemann, W., 2005, *Worship in Ancient Israel: An Essential Guide*, Nashville, TN: Abingdon Press.

Brueggemann, W., 2014, *From Whom No Secrets Are Hid: Introducing the Psalms*, Louisville, KY: Westminster John Knox Press.

Burkett, D., 1999, *The Son of Man Debate: A History and Evaluation*, Cambridge: Cambridge University Press.

Carroll, R. P., 1979, *When Prophecy Failed: Reactions and Responses to Failure in the Old Testament Prophetic Traditions*, London: SCM Press.

Cary, P., 2008, *Jonah* (SCM Theological Commentaries), London: SCM Press.

Ceresko, A. R., 1992, *Introduction to the Old Testament: A Liberation Perspective*, London: Geoffrey Chapman.

Childs, B. S., 1985, *Introduction to the Old Testament as Scripture*, Philadelphia, PA: Fortress Press.

Clines, D., 1995, *Interested Parties: The Ideology of Writers and Readers of the Hebrew Bible*, Sheffield: Sheffield Academic Press.

Clines, D., 1996, *The Theme of the Pentateuch*, Sheffield: Sheffield Academic Press.

Coggins, R., 1990, *Introducing the Old Testament*, Oxford: Oxford University Press.

Cone, J. H., 1997, *God of the Oppressed*, London: SPCK.

Cox, H. and Paulsell, S., 2012, *Lamentations and the Song of Songs* (Belief Commentaries), Louisville, KY: Westminster John Knox Press.

Davidson, R., 1983, *The Courage to Doubt: Exploring an Old Testament Theme*, London: SCM Press.

Davies, P. R., 1992, *In Search of 'Ancient Israel'*, Sheffield: Sheffield Academic Press.

Davis, E. F., 2014, *Biblical Prophecy: Perspectives for Christian Theology, Discipleship and Ministry*, Louisville, KY: Westminster John Knox Press.

Day, J. (ed.), 2004, *In Search of Pre-Exilic Israel*, London: T. & T. Clark.

Dever, W., 2001, *What Did the Biblical Writers Know and When Did They Know It?* Cambridge: Eerdmans.

Dever, W., 2003, *Who Were the Early Israelites and Where Did They Come From?* Cambridge: Eerdmans.

Douglas, M., 1966, *Purity and Danger: An Analysis of the Concepts of Pollution and Taboo*, London: Routledge.

Eaton, J. H., 1985, *Job*, Sheffield: JSOT Press.

Eichrodt, W., 1964, *Theology of the Old Testament* (trans. J. Barton), London: SCM Press.

Fritz, V., 1994, *An Introduction to Biblical Archaeology*, Sheffield: Sheffield Academic Press.

Gerstenberger, E. S., 2001, 'The Psalter', in L. G. Perdue (ed.), *The Blackwell Companion to the Hebrew Bible*, Oxford: Blackwell, pp. 402–17.

Gerstenberger, E. S., 2002, *Theologies in the Old Testament*, London: T. & T. Clark.

Gooder, P., 2000, *The Pentateuch: A Story of Beginnings*, London: Continuum.

Gottwald, N., 1979, *The Tribes of Yahweh: A Sociology of the Religion of Liberated Israel 1250–1050 B.C.E.*, London: SCM Press.

Gowan, D. E., 1976, *Bridge Between the Testaments*, Pittsburgh, PA: Pickwick Press.

Gowan, D. E., 2000, *Eschatology in the Old Testament*, Edinburgh: T. & T. Clark.

Gowan, D. E., 2001, *Daniel* (Abingdon Old Testament Commentaries), Nashville, TN: Abingdon Press.

Gunkel, H. (1933) 1998, *An Introduction to the Psalms: The Genres of the Religious Lyric of Israel* (trans. J. D. Nogalski), Macon, GA: Mercer University Press.

Gunn, D. M. and Fewell, D. N., 1993, *Narrative in the Hebrew Bible*, Oxford: Oxford University Press.

Heaton, E. W., 1996, *A Short Introduction to the Old Testament Prophets*, Oxford: One World.

Holdsworth, J., 2005, *SCM Studyguide to the Old Testament*, London: SCM Press.

Holdsworth, J., 2010, *Lies, Sex and Politicians: Communicating the Old Testament in Contemporary Culture*, London: SCM Press.

Jarick, J., 2002, *1 Chronicles*, Sheffield: Sheffield Academic Press.

Kirsch, J., 1997, *The Harlot by the Side of the Road*, London: Rider Books.

Klein, R. W., 2001, 'Narrative Texts: Chronicles, Ezra and Nehemiah', in L. G. Perdue (ed.), *The Blackwell Companion to the Hebrew Bible*, Oxford: Blackwell, pp. 385–401.

Larkin, K. J. A., 1995, *Ruth and Esther* (Old Testament Guides), Sheffield: Sheffield Academic Press.

Lemche, N. P., 1998, *The Israelites in History and Tradition*, London: SPCK.

Lindars, B., 1961, *New Testament Apologetic: The Doctrinal Significance of the Old Testament Quotations*, London: SCM Press.

Lohfink, N., 1994, *Theology of the Pentateuch: Themes of the Priestly Narrative and Deuteronomy*, Edinburgh: T. & T. Clark.

Mason, R., 1997, *Propaganda and Subversion in the Old Testament*, London: SPCK.

McGrath, A. E., 2003, *A Brief History of Heaven*, Oxford: Blackwell.

Mendenhall, G. E., 1962, 'The Hebrew Conquest of Palestine', *Biblical Archaeologist* 25/3, pp. 66–87.

Mendenhall, G. E., 2001, *Ancient Israel's Faith and History: An Introduction to the Bible in Context*, Louisville, KY: Westminster John Knox Press.

Meyers, C., 2001, 'Early Israel and the Rise of the Israelite Monarchy', in L. G. Perdue (ed.), *The Blackwell Companion to the Hebrew Bible*, Oxford: Blackwell, pp. 385–401.

Meyers, C., 2005, *Exodus* (The New Cambridge Bible Commentary), Cambridge: Cambridge University Press.

Miles, J., 1995, *God: A Biography*, London: Simon & Schuster.

Miller, P. D., 2013, *The Lord of the Psalms*, Louisville, KY: Westminster John Knox Press.

Mills, M. E., 1998, *Images of God in the Old Testament*, London: Cassell.

Mills, M. E., 1999, *Historical Israel: Biblical Israel: Studying Joshua to 2 Kings*, London: Cassell.

Mills, M. E., 2001, *Biblical Morality: Moral Perspectives in Old Testament Narratives*, Aldershot: Ashgate.

Mowinckel, S., 1967, *The Psalms in Israel's Worship* (trans. D. R. Ap-Thomas), 2 vols, Oxford: Blackwell.

Noth, M., 1960, *The History of Israel* (trans. S. Godman), 2nd edn (revised trans. P. R. Ackroyd), London: A. & C. Black.

O'Connor, K. M., 2003, *Lamentations and the Tears of the World*, Maryknoll, NY: Orbis Books.

Perdue, L. G. (ed.), 2001, *The Blackwell Companion to the Hebrew Bible*, Oxford: Blackwell.

Prévost, J.-P., 1993, *How to Read the Apocalypse*, London: SCM Press.

Prévost, J.-P., 1996, *How to Read the Prophets*, London: SCM Press.

Robinson, J. A. T., 1957, *Jesus and his Coming: The Emergence of a Doctrine*, London: SCM Press.

Rodd, C., 2001, *Glimpses of a Strange Land: Studies in Old Testament Ethics*, Edinburgh: T. & T. Clark.

Rogerson, J., 2004, *Genesis 1—11*, T. & T. Clark Study Guides, London: T. & T. Clark.

Russell, D. S., 1964, *The Method and Message of Jewish Apocalyptic*, London: SCM Press.

Ryle, H. E., 1909, *The Canon of the Old Testament*, London: Macmillan.

Sawyer, J. F. A., 1993, *Prophecy and the Biblical Prophets*, Oxford: Oxford University Press.

Schofield, J. N., 1969, *Law, Prophets, and Writings: The Religion of the Books of the Old Testament*, London: SPCK.

Smith-Christopher, D., 2002, *A Biblical Theology of Exile*, Minneapolis, MN: Fortress Press.

Smith-Christopher, D., 2007, *Jonah, Jesus, and Other Good Coyotes: Speaking Peace to Power in the Bible*, Nashville, TN: Abingdon Press.

Snaith, N. H. (1944) 1997, *The Distinctive Ideas of the Old Testament*, Carlisle: Paternoster Press.

Trible, P., 1984, *Texts of Terror*, London: SCM Press.

Van Wolde, E., 1997, *Mr and Mrs Job*, London: SCM Press.

Von Rad, G., 1963, *Old Testament Theology, Vol. 1: The Theology of Israel's Historical Traditions*, London: Oliver & Boyd.

Von Rad, G., 1966, *Deuteronomy: A Commentary*, London: SCM Press.

Wellhausen, J., (1885) 2003, *Prolegomena to the History of Ancient Israel*, Eugene, OR: Wipf & Stock.

Wenham, G. J., 2000, *Story as Torah*, Edinburgh: T. & T. Clark.

Westermann, C., 1981, *Praise and Lament in the Psalms* (trans. K. R. Crim and R. N. Soulen), Atlanta, GA: John Knox Press.

Whitelam, K. W., 1996, *The Invention of Ancient Israel: The Silencing of Palestinian History*, London: Routledge.

Whybray, R. N., 1998, *Job*, Sheffield: Sheffield Academic Press.

Williamson, H. G. M., 1985, *Ezra Nehemiah* (Word Biblical Commentary), Waco, TX: Word Books.

Williamson, H. G. M., 1987, *Ezra and Nehemiah* (Old Testament Guides), Sheffield: Sheffield Academic Press.